Bible Promises
to Treasure

for Mom

Bible Promises
to Treasure

Inspiring

words

for every

occasion

BROADMAN
&HOLMAN
PUBLISHERS

Nashville, Tennessee

Bible Promises to Treasure for Mom
© 1998 Broadman & Holman Publishers,
Nashville, Tennessee
All rights reserved
Printed in Belgium

ISBN# 1–55819–711–7

Dewey Decimal Classification: 306.87
Subject Heading: MOTHERS
Library of Congress Card Catalog Number: 97–25916

******

A note on the sources of quotations. When possible I have supplied at least the book name from which contemporary quotes have come. Yet even this is often impossible, since many came from my "journal of jottings" over many years. Also, if a quote is from a person who lived longer than fifty or so years ago, I've made no attempt to cite the source. Such quotations are usually available in any standard book of quotes.

******

All Scripture passages are from the Authorized King James Version.

Library of Congress Cataloging-in-Publication Data
Bible promises to treasure for mom / compiled by Gary Wilde.
    p. cm.
    Includes bibliographical references.
    ISBN 1–55819–711–7 (hc)
        1. Mothers—Religious life—Quotations, maxims, etc..
2. Motherhood—Religious aspects—Christianity—Quotations,
maxims, etc.
    I. Wilde, Gary.
BV4847.P76   1998
248.8'431—dc21

                                                            97–25916
                                                                CIP

3 4 5 6   02 01 00 99

Contents

v

Introduction

I remember as a child singing often at church: "Standing on the Promises of God." Or maybe it was mostly the adults who were singing; but I was standing next to them—my parents and all the others. I recall those faithful people joyfully reciting words they must surely have known by heart . . .

**When the howling storms
of doubt and fear assail,
By the living Word of God I shall prevail,
Standing on the promises of God.**

For years Downey Church, in sunny central Florida, had preached and taught the promises of God and believed in His goodness. From the beginning—when the church building was a small tin-roofed, A-frame at the east end of a dirt road on the outskirts of Orlando—people would gather to stand on the immutable promises. Under the shiny tin roof, standing on the sandy-wooden floorboards, they melded their voices to the tunes of the upright piano and recalled God's goodness. Today, as the church there grows and thrives—now there is also a school and gymnasium—I can only attribute its vibrant life to a love of God's promises and the recognition that without the pledges that flow from the mouth of God, there is no church, no music, and no reason for either.

The promises of God have always been the bedrock of Christian faith; for without God's sacred covenants with us, we cannot survive. In times of joy or heartache, in all our ups and downs, we keep coming back to that source of our life: the motivation for all our doing and the reason for our existence. It is the message of God's mighty assurances: this life is not all there is, He will always be with us while we are here, and He will take us to be with Him someday. Yes, we do have priceless promises to keep close to our hearts!

My hope for you as you delve into this scriptural treasure chest is that you will grow deeper in love with the One who has spoken as no other ever could. With so many influences bombarding our minds each moment of the day, what could be better than to set aside a few moments of quiet to hear the still, small voice that constantly invites us into warm fellowship? We'll be richly rewarded if we truly listen to what that voice is saying. His words convey blessing and guidance, wisdom and warning, life for now and life everlasting. What incomparable grace!

Gary Wilde
Colorado Springs, 1997

One

Keeping Close to the Lord

Being a good mom requires more than pure self-effort. It means relying upon the One who gives us our life with the dawning of each new day. Though it's so easy to forget that He makes His home in our hearts, we can seek moments of quietness, throughout the day, to recognize His closeness. Let these words from the Word make you aware of His presence.

Pursuing the Knowledge of God

Begin and end the day with him
who is the Alpha and Omega,
and if you really experience what it is
to love God, you will redeem
all the time you can
for his more immediate service.

—*Susanna Wesley*

Be still, and know that I am God:
I will be exalted among the heathen,
I will be exalted in the earth.

—*Psalm 46:10*

Then Paul stood in the midst of Mars' hill, and said, Ye men of Athens, I perceive that in all things ye are too superstitious.

For as I passed by, and beheld your devotions, I found an altar with this inscription, TO THE UNKNOWN GOD. Whom therefore ye ignorantly worship, him declare I unto you.

God that made the world and all things therein, seeing that he is Lord of heaven and earth, dwelleth not in temples made with hands;

Neither is worshipped with men's hands, as though he needed any thing, seeing he giveth to all life, and breath, and all things;

And hath made of one blood all nations of men for to dwell on all the face of the earth, and hath determined the times before appointed, and the bounds of their habitation;

That they should seek the Lord, if haply they might feel after him, and find him, though he be not far from every one of us.

—Acts 17:22–27

Hearing His Word

Who is he, that all my faculties should thus obey him? Who is he that gives light in such darkness in a moment; who softens a heart that seemed made of stone; who gives the waters of sweet tears, where for a long time great dryness seems to have prevailed; who inspires these desires; who bestows this courage? . . . I desire to serve this my Lord; I aim at nothing else but his pleasure; I seek no joy, no rest, no other good than that of doing his will.

—*Teresa of Avila*

Thy word have I hid in mine heart, that I might not sin against thee. . . .

I will delight myself in thy statutes: I will not forget thy word. . . .

So shall I have wherewith to answer him that reproacheth me: for I trust in thy word. . . .

This is my comfort in my affliction: for thy word hath quickened me.

—*Psalm 119:11, 16, 42, 50*

All scripture is given by inspiration of God, and is profitable for doctrine, for reproof, for correction, for instruction in righteousness:

That the man of God may be perfect, throughly furnished unto all good works.

—*2 Timothy 3:16–17*

For the word of God is quick, and powerful, and sharper than any two-edged sword, piercing even to the dividing asunder of soul and spirit, and of the joints and marrow, and is a discerner of the thoughts and intents of the heart.

Neither is there any creature that is not manifest in his sight: but all things are naked and opened unto the eyes of him with whom we have to do.

—*Hebrews 4:12–13*

Overcoming Your Doubts . . .

We do not need the sheltering wings when things go smoothly. We are closest to God in the darkness, stumbling along blindly.

—Madeleine L'Engle[1]

Have not I commanded thee? Be strong and of a good courage; be not afraid, neither be thou dismayed: for the LORD thy God is with thee whithersoever thou goest.

—Joshua 1:9

Behold, I am the LORD, the God of all flesh: is there any thing too hard for me?

—Jeremiah 32:27

For with God nothing shall be impossible.

—Luke 1:37

For we walk by faith, not by sight.

—2 Corinthians 5:7

[Have] your feet shod with the preparation of the gospel of peace;

Above all, taking the shield of faith, wherewith ye shall be able to quench all the fiery darts of the wicked.

—Ephesians 6:15–16

Trusting His Promises . . .

The highest pinnacle of the spiritual life is not joy in unbroken sunshine but absolute and undoubting trust in the love of God.

—A.W. Thorold

If thou wilt diligently hearken to the voice of the LORD thy God, and wilt do that which is right in his sight, and wilt give ear to his commandments, and keep all his statutes, I will put none of these diseases upon thee, which I have brought upon the Egyptians: for I am the LORD that healeth thee.

—Exodus 15:26

For verily I say unto you, That whosoever shall say unto this mountain, Be thou removed, and be thou cast into the sea; and shall not doubt in his heart, but shall believe that those things which he saith shall come to pass; he shall have whatsoever he saith.

—*Mark 11:23*

Let us hold fast the profession of our faith without wavering; (for he is faithful that promised. . . .

Cast not away therefore your confidence, which hath great recompence of reward.

For ye have need of patience, that, after ye have done the will of God, ye might receive the promise.

For yet a little while, and he that shall come will come, and will not tarry.

—*Hebrews 10:23, 35–37*

And this is the confidence that we have in him, that, if we ask any thing according to his will, he heareth us:

And if we know that he hear us, whatsoever we ask, we know that we have the petitions that we desired of him.

—*1 John 5:14–15*

⋘ *For Daily Protection*

The angel of the LORD encampeth round about them that fear him, and delivereth them.

—*Psalm 34:7*

When thou passest through the waters, I will be with thee; and through the rivers, they shall not overflow thee: when thou walkest through the fire, thou shalt not be burned; neither shall the flame kindle upon thee.

—*Isaiah 43:2*

Fear not them which kill the body, but are not able to kill the soul: but rather fear him which is able to destroy both soul and body in hell.

Are not two sparrows sold for a farthing? and one of them shall not fall on the ground without your Father.

But the very hairs of your head are all numbered.

Fear ye not therefore, ye are of more value than many sparrows.

—*Matthew 10:28–31*

❦ *For Joy in Living*

The LORD is the portion of mine inheritance and of my cup: thou maintainest my lot.

The lines are fallen unto me in pleasant places; yea, I have a goodly heritage.

—Psalm 16:5–6

Thou hast turned for me my mourning into dancing: thou hast put off my sackcloth, and girded me with gladness;

To the end that my glory may sing praise to thee, and not be silent. O LORD my God, I will give thanks unto thee for ever.

—Psalm 30:11–12

He maketh the barren woman to keep house, and to be a joyful mother of children. Praise ye the LORD.

—Psalm 113:9

They that sow in tears shall reap in joy.

He that goeth forth and weepeth, bearing precious seed, shall doubtless come again with rejoicing, bringing his sheaves with him.

—Psalm 126:5–6

Sing, O ye heavens; for the LORD hath done it: shout, ye lower parts of the earth: break forth into singing, ye mountains, O forest, and every tree therein: for the LORD hath redeemed Jacob, and glorified himself in Israel.

—Isaiah 44:23

Thou hast loved righteousness, and hated iniquity; therefore God, even thy God, hath anointed thee with the oil of gladness above thy fellows.

—Hebrews 1:9

My brethren, count it all joy when ye fall into divers temptations;

Knowing this, that the trying of your faith worketh patience.

But let patience have her perfect work, that ye may be perfect and entire, wanting nothing.

If any of you lack wisdom, let him ask of God, that giveth to all men liberally, and upbraideth not; and it shall be given him.

But let him ask in faith, nothing wavering. For he that wavereth is like a wave of the sea driven with the wind and tossed.

—James 1:2–6

But rejoice, inasmuch as ye are partakers of Christ's sufferings; that, when his glory shall be revealed, ye may be glad also with exceeding joy.

—1 Peter 4:13

⋘ *For Eternity*

For surely there is an end; and thine expectation shall not be cut off.

—Proverbs 23:18

He hath made every thing beautiful in his time: also he hath set the world in their heart, so that no man can find out the work that God maketh from the beginning to the end.

—Ecclesiastes 3:11

Thus saith the LORD the King of Israel, and his redeemer the LORD of hosts; I am the first, and I am the last; and beside me there is no God.

—Isaiah 44:6

I am Alpha and Omega, the beginning and the ending, saith the Lord, which is, and which was, and which is to come, the Almighty. . . . I am he that liveth, and was

dead; and, behold, I am alive for evermore,
Amen; and have the keys of hell and of death.

—Revelation 1:8, 18

Accepting His "Food"

*As I take the bread and the cup, I find new
strength and increased vigor coming into my
life. With the bread, I look back in penitence
and thank Him for His forgivness. With the
cup, I look forward and thank Him for His
promise of strength for whatever comes. As I
rise from this place, let me set out anew to
follow Him wherever He leads.*

—E. Paul Hovey [2]

As they were eating, Jesus took bread, and
blessed it, and brake it, and gave it to the disciples, and said, Take, eat; this is my body.

And he took the cup, and gave thanks, and
gave it to them, saying, Drink ye all of it;

For this is my blood of the new testament,
which is shed for many for the remission of sins.

—Matthew 26:26–28

Labour not for the meat which perisheth, but for that meat which endureth unto everlasting life, which the Son of man shall give unto you: for him hath God the Father sealed.

Then said they unto him, What shall we do, that we might work the works of God?

Jesus answered and said unto them, This is the work of God, that ye believe on him whom he hath sent.

They said therefore unto him, What sign shewest thou then, that we may see, and believe thee? what dost thou work?

Our fathers did eat manna in the desert; as it is written, He gave them bread from heaven to eat.

Then Jesus said unto them, Verily, verily, I say unto you, Moses gave you not that bread from heaven; but my Father giveth you the true bread from heaven.

For the bread of God is he which cometh down from heaven, and giveth life unto the world.

Then said they unto him, Lord, evermore give us this bread.

And Jesus said unto them, I am the bread of life: he that cometh to me shall never hunger; and he that believeth on me shall never thirst.

—John 6:27–34

I am the living bread which came down from heaven: if any man eat of this bread, he shall live for ever: and the bread that I will give is my flesh, which I will give for the life of the world.

The Jews therefore strove among themselves, saying, How can this man give us his flesh to eat?

Then Jesus said unto them, Verily, verily, I say unto you, Except ye eat the flesh of the Son of man, and drink his blood, ye have no life in you.

Whoso eateth my flesh, and drinketh my blood, hath eternal life; and I will raise him up at the last day.

For my flesh is meat indeed, and my blood is drink indeed.

He that eateth my flesh, and drinketh my blood, dwelleth in me, and I in him.

As the living Father hath sent me, and I live by the Father: so he that eateth me, even he shall live by me.

This is that bread which came down from heaven: not as your fathers did eat manna, and are dead: he that eateth of this bread shall live for ever.

—John 6:51–58

The cup of blessing which we bless, is it not the communion of the blood of Christ? The bread which we break, is it not the communion of the body of Christ?

For we being many are one bread, and one body: for we are all partakers of that one bread. . . . Whether therefore ye eat, or drink, or whatsoever ye do, do all to the glory of God.

—*1 Corinthians 10:16–17, 31*

Enjoying His Blessings

God, of thy goodness, give me thyself;
for thou art enough to me.

—*Julian of Norwich*

But whoso hearkeneth unto me shall dwell safely, and shall be quiet from fear of evil.

—*Proverbs 1:33*

Why sayest thou, O Jacob, and speakest, O Israel, My way is hid from the LORD, and my judgment is passed over from my God?

Hast thou not known? hast thou not heard, that the everlasting God, the LORD, the Creator of the ends of the earth, fainteth not, neither is weary? there is no searching of his understanding.

—Isaiah 40:27–28

Who is a God like unto thee, that pardoneth iniquity, and passeth by the transgression of the remnant of his heritage? he retaineth not his anger for ever, because he delighteth in mercy.

He will turn again, he will have compassion upon us; he will subdue our iniquities; and thou wilt cast all their sins into the depths of the sea.

—Micah 7:18–19

Ask ye of the LORD rain in the time of the latter rain; so the LORD shall make bright clouds, and give them showers of rain, to every one grass in the field.

—Zechariah 10:1

Be not ye therefore like unto them: for your Father knoweth what things ye have need of, before ye ask him. . . . Take therefore no thought for the morrow: for the morrow shall take thought for the things of itself. Sufficient unto the day is the evil thereof.

—Matthew 6:8, 34

If ye abide in me, and my words abide in you, ye shall ask what ye will, and it shall be done unto you.

—John 15:7

Hitherto have ye asked nothing in my name: ask, and ye shall receive, that your joy may be full.

—John 16:24

Are ye so foolish? having begun in the Spirit, are ye now made perfect by the flesh?

Have ye suffered so many things in vain? if it be yet in vain. . . . . But now, after that ye have known God, or rather are known of God, how turn ye again to the weak and beggarly elements, whereunto ye desire again to be in bondage?

Ye observe days, and months, and times, and years.

I am afraid of you, lest I have bestowed upon you labour in vain.

—Galatians 3:3–4; 4:9–11

Stand fast therefore in the liberty wherewith Christ hath made us free, and be not
entangled again with the yoke of bondage.

—*Galatians 5:1*

Having therefore, brethren, boldness to
enter into the holiest by the blood of Jesus,
By a new and living way, which he hath
consecrated for us, through the veil, that is to
say, his flesh;
And having an high priest over the house
of God;
Let us draw near with a true heart in full
assurance of faith, having our hearts sprinkled from an evil conscience, and our bodies
washed with pure water.

—*Hebrews 10:19–22*

Now unto him that is able to do exceeding
abundantly above all that we ask or think,
according to the power that worketh in us.

—*Ephesians 3:20*

Loving Your Children

Most of the time it's easy to love our children. They're so cute . . . or acting so "grown up" . . . or being so successful. But what about the other times? When children clearly fail to meet our expectations? That's when the Word can help us pursue an attitude of unconditional love, offering the same kind of grace that God extends to us.

Recognize the Value of Every Child

I do not believe in a child world. . . . I believe the child should be taught from the very first that the whole world is his world, that adult and child share one world, that all generations are needed.

—*Pearl S. Buck* [1]

And they have cast lots for my people; and have given a boy for an harlot, and sold a girl for wine, that they might drink.

—*Joel 3:3*

At the same time came the disciples unto Jesus, saying, Who is the greatest in the kingdom of heaven?

And Jesus called a little child unto him, and set him in the midst of them,

And said, Verily I say unto you, Except ye be converted, and become as little children, ye shall not enter into the kingdom of heaven.

Whosoever therefore shall humble himself as this little child, the same is greatest in the kingdom of heaven

And whoso shall receive one such little child in my name receiveth me.

But whoso shall offend one of these little ones which believe in me, it were better for him that a millstone were hanged about his neck, and that he were drowned in the depth of the sea.

—Matthew 18:1–6

Then were there brought unto him little children, that he should put his hands on them, and pray: and the disciples rebuked them.

But Jesus said, Suffer little children, and forbid them not, to come unto me: for of such is the kingdom of heaven.

And he laid his hands on them, and departed thence.

—Matthew 19:13–15

And he took a child, and set him in the midst of them: and when he had taken him in his arms, he said unto them,

Whosoever shall receive one of such children in my name, receiveth me: and whosoever shall receive me, receiveth not me, but him that sent me.

—*Mark 9:36–37*

And they brought unto him also infants, that he would touch them: but when his disciples saw it, they rebuked them.

But Jesus called them unto him, and said, Suffer little children to come unto me, and forbid them not: for of such is the kingdom of God.

Verily I say unto you, Whosoever shall not receive the kingdom of God as a little child shall in no wise enter therein.

—*Luke 18:15–17*

Behold, the third time I am ready to come to you; and I will not be burdensome to you: for I seek not yours, but you: for the children ought not to lay up for the parents, but the parents for the children.

—*2 Corinthians 12:14*

Cherish Your Children

You realize that your home is as you like it when you overhear a six-year-old hostess tell a little guest, "Don't worry about making noise. Our Mommie and Daddy like children."

—Burton Hillis [2]

Like as a father pitieth his children, so the LORD pitieth them that fear him.

For he knoweth our frame; he remembereth that we are dust.

—Psalm 103:13–14

He maketh the barren woman to keep house, and to be a joyful mother of children. Praise ye the LORD.

—Psalm 113:9

Lo, children are an heritage of the LORD: and the fruit of the womb is his reward.

As arrows are in the hand of a mighty man; so are children of the youth.

Happy is the man that hath his quiver full of them: they shall not be ashamed, but they shall speak with the enemies in the gate.

—Psalm 127:3–5

Help Them Know God and His Wisdom

He who helps a child helps humanity with a distinctness, with an immediateness which no other help given to human creatures in any other stage of their human life can possible give again.

—*Phillips Brooks*

Doth not wisdom cry? and understanding put forth her voice?

She standeth in the top of high places, by the way in the places of the paths.

She crieth at the gates, at the entry of the city, at the coming in at the doors.

Unto you, O men, I call; and my voice is to the sons of man.

O ye simple, understand wisdom: and, ye fools, be ye of an understanding heart.

Hear; for I will speak of excellent things; and the opening of my lips shall be right things.

For my mouth shall speak truth; and wickedness is an abomination to my lips.

All the words of my mouth are in righteousness; there is nothing froward or perverse in them.

—Proverbs 8:1–8

I beseech you therefore, brethren, by the mercies of God, that ye present your bodies a living sacrifice, holy, acceptable unto God, which is your reasonable service.

And be not conformed to this world: but be ye transformed by the renewing of your mind, that ye may prove what is that good, and acceptable, and perfect, will of God.

—Romans 12:1–2

If ye then be risen with Christ, seek those things which are above, where Christ sitteth on the right hand of God.

Set your affection on things above, not on things on the earth.

For ye are dead, and your life is hid with Christ in God.

—Colossians 3:1–3

But be ye doers of the word, and not hearers only, deceiving your own selves.

For if any be a hearer of the word, and not a doer, he is like unto a man beholding his natural face in a glass:

For he beholdeth himself, and goeth his way, and straightway forgetteth what manner of man he was.

But whoso looketh into the perfect law of liberty, and continueth therein, he being not a forgetful hearer, but a doer of the work, this man shall be blessed in his deed.

If any man among you seem to be religious, and bridleth not his tongue, but deceiveth his own heart, this man's religion is vain.

Pure religion and undefiled before God and the Father is this, To visit the fatherless and widows in their affliction, and to keep himself unspotted from the world.

—*James 1:22–27*

Bless Your Children, and Envision Their Future

When I approach a child,
he inspires in me two sentiments:
tenderness for what he is,
and respect for what he may become.
—Louis Pasteur

And God blessed them, saying, Be fruitful, and multiply, and fill the waters in the seas, and let fowl multiply in the earth.

—*Genesis 1:22*

His father Isaac said unto him, Come near now, and kiss me, my son.

And he came near, and kissed him: and he smelled the smell of his raiment, and blessed him, and said, See, the smell of my son is as the smell of a field which the LORD hath blessed:

Therefore God give thee of the dew of heaven, and the fatness of the earth, and plenty of corn and wine:

Let people serve thee, and nations bow
down to thee: be lord over thy brethren, and
let thy mother's sons bow down to thee:
cursed be every one that curseth thee, and
blessed be he that blesseth thee.

—Genesis 27:26–29

And Israel beheld Joseph's sons, and said,
Who are these?

And Joseph said unto his father, They are
my sons, whom God hath given me in this
place. And he said, Bring them, I pray thee,
unto me, and I will bless them.

Now the eyes of Israel were dim for age, so
that he could not see. And he brought them
near unto him; and he kissed them, and
embraced them.

And Israel said unto Joseph, I had not
thought to see thy face: and, lo, God hath
shewed me also thy seed.

And Joseph brought them out from
between his knees, and he bowed himself with
his face to the earth.

And Joseph took them both, Ephraim in
his right hand toward Israel's left hand, and
Manasseh in his left hand toward Israel's right
hand, and brought them near unto him.

And Israel stretched out his right hand, and laid it upon Ephraim's head, who was the younger, and his left hand upon Manasseh's head, guiding his hands wittingly; for Manasseh was the firstborn.

And he blessed Joseph, and said, God, before whom my fathers Abraham and Isaac did walk, the God which fed me all my life long unto this day,

The Angel which redeemed me from all evil, bless the lads; and let my name be named on them, and the name of my fathers Abraham and Isaac; and let them grow into a multitude in the midst of the earth.

—Genesis 48:8–16

Speak unto Aaron and unto his sons, saying, On this wise ye shall bless the children of Israel, saying unto them,

The LORD bless thee, and keep thee:

The LORD make his face shine upon thee, and be gracious unto thee:

The LORD lift up his countenance upon thee, and give thee peace.

—Numbers 6:23–26

Naomi said unto her two daughters in law, Go, return each to her mother's house: the LORD deal kindly with you, as ye have dealt with the dead, and with me.

The LORD grant you that ye may find rest, each of you in the house of her husband. Then she kissed them; and they lifted up their voice, and wept.

—*Ruth 1:8–9*

And he led them out as far as to Bethany, and he lifted up his hands, and blessed them.

And it came to pass, while he blessed them, he was parted from them, and carried up into heaven.

And they worshipped him, and returned to Jerusalem with great joy:

And were continually in the temple, praising and blessing God. Amen.

—*Luke 24:50–53*

Be Their Best Example!

There is nothing more influential in a child's life than the moral power of quiet example. For children to take morality seriously they must see adults take morality seriously.

—*William Bennett*[3]

Ye shall not afflict any widow, or fatherless child.

If thou afflict them in any wise, and they cry at all unto me, I will surely hear their cry.

—*Exodus 22:22–23*

Only take heed to thyself, and keep thy soul diligently, lest thou forget the things which thine eyes have seen, and lest they depart from thy heart all the days of thy life: but teach them thy sons, and thy sons' sons;

Specially the day that thou stoodest before the LORD thy God in Horeb, when the LORD said unto me, Gather me the people together, and I will make them hear my words, that they may learn to fear me all the days that they shall live upon the earth, and that they may teach their children.

—*Deuteronomy 4:9–10*

And ye shall teach them your children, speaking of them when thou sittest in thine house, and when thou walkest by the way, when thou liest down, and when thou risest up.

—*Deuteronomy 11:19*

There came a man of God unto Eli, and said unto him, Thus saith the LORD, Did I plainly appear unto the house of thy father, when they were in Egypt in Pharaoh's house?

And did I choose him out of all the tribes of Israel to be my priest, to offer upon mine altar, to burn incense, to wear an ephod before me? and did I give unto the house of thy father all the offerings made by fire of the children of Israel?

Wherefore kick ye at my sacrifice and at mine offering, which I have commanded in my habitation; and honourest thy sons above me, to make yourselves fat with the chiefest of all the offerings of Israel my people?

Wherefore the LORD God of Israel saith, I said indeed that thy house, and the house of thy father, should walk before me for ever: but now the LORD saith, Be it far from me; for them that honour me I will honour, and they that despise me shall be lightly esteemed.

Behold, the days come, that I will cut off thine arm, and the arm of thy father's house, that there shall not be an old man in thine house.

And thou shalt see an enemy in my habitation, in all the wealth which God shall give Israel: and there shall not be an old man in thine house for ever.

And the man of thine, whom I shall not cut off from mine altar, shall be to consume thine eyes, and to grieve thine heart: and all the increase of thine house shall die in the flower of their age.

And this shall be a sign unto thee, that shall come upon thy two sons, on Hophni and Phinehas; in one day they shall die both of them.

—*1 Samuel 2:27–34*

Thou hast seen it; for thou beholdest mischief and spite, to requite it with thy hand: the poor committeth himself unto thee; thou art the helper of the fatherless.

Break thou the arm of the wicked and the evil man: seek out his wickedness till thou find none.

The LORD is King for ever and ever: the heathen are perished out of his land.

LORD, thou hast heard the desire of the humble: thou wilt prepare their hearts, thou wilt cause thine ear to hear:

To judge the fatherless and the oppressed, that the man of the earth may no more oppress.

—*Psalm 10:14–18*

And it shall come to pass, when thou shalt shew this people all these words, and they shall say unto thee, Wherefore hath the LORD pronounced all this great evil against us? or what is our iniquity? or what is our sin that we have committed against the LORD our God?

Then shalt thou say unto them, Because your fathers have forsaken me, saith the LORD, and have walked after other gods, and have served them, and have worshipped them, and have forsaken me, and have not kept my law;

And ye have done worse than your fathers; for, behold, ye walk every one after the imagination of his evil heart, that they may not hearken unto me:

Therefore will I cast you out of this land into a land that ye know not, neither ye nor your fathers; and there shall ye serve other gods day and night; where I will not shew you favour.

—*Jeremiah 16:10–13*

Remember: God Works through Children, Too!

Each child is unique, a special creation of God with talents, abilities, personality, preferences, dislikes, potentials, strengths, weaknesses, and skills that are his or her own. As parents, we must seek to identify these in each of our children and help them become the persons God intended.

—*Dave Veerman* [4]

And the child Samuel ministered unto the LORD before Eli. And the word of the LORD was precious in those days; there was no open vision.

And it came to pass at that time, when Eli was laid down in his place, and his eyes began to wax dim, that he could not see;

And ere the lamp of God went out in the temple of the LORD, where the ark of God was, and Samuel was laid down to sleep;

That the LORD called Samuel: and he answered, Here am I.

And he ran unto Eli, and said, Here am I; for thou calledst me. And he said, I called not; lie down again. And he went and lay down.

And the LORD called yet again, Samuel. And Samuel arose and went to Eli, and said, Here am I; for thou didst call me. And he answered, I called not, my son; lie down again.

Now Samuel did not yet know the LORD, neither was the word of the LORD yet revealed unto him.

And the LORD called Samuel again the third time. And he arose and went to Eli, and said, Here am I; for thou didst call me. And Eli perceived that the LORD had called the child.

Therefore Eli said unto Samuel, Go, lie down: and it shall be, if he call thee, that thou shalt say, Speak, LORD; for thy servant heareth. So Samuel went and lay down in his place.

And the LORD came, and stood, and called as at other times, Samuel, Samuel. Then Samuel answered, Speak; for thy servant heareth.

And the LORD said to Samuel, Behold, I will do a thing in Israel, at which both the ears of every one that heareth it shall tingle.

In that day I will perform against Eli all things which I have spoken concerning his house: when I begin, I will also make an end.

For I have told him that I will judge his house for ever for the iniquity which he knoweth; because his sons made themselves vile, and he restrained them not.

And therefore I have sworn unto the house of Eli, that the iniquity of Eli's house shall not be purged with sacrifice nor offering for ever.

—*1 Samuel 3:1–14*

—Three—

Guiding Your Children

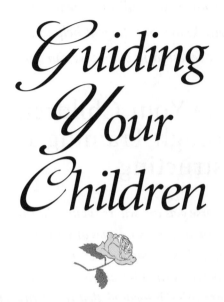

There have been times in history when the experts thought it best to let children develop "naturally." If simply left to their own choices, youngsters would grow into free and happy adults.

Few would subscribe to such a theory today. And it's certainly not a biblical approach! God calls us to train and instruct our children from their earliest days. They need our guidance—and want it with all their hearts. For, as they secretly know, our diligent help and correction is the deepest form of love we can offer.

Love Your Children through Training and Instructing

No horse gets anywhere till he is harnessed. No steam or gas ever drives anything until it is confined. No Niagara is ever turned into light and power until it is tunneled. No life ever grows great until it is focused, dedicated, disciplined.

—Harry Emerson Fosdick

Train up a child in the way he should go: and when he is old, he will not depart from it.

—Proverbs 22:6

Correct thy son, and he shall give thee rest; yea, he shall give delight unto thy soul.

—Proverbs 29:17

Only take heed to thyself, and keep thy soul diligently, lest thou forget the things which thine eyes have seen, and lest they depart from thy heart all the days of thy life: but teach them thy sons, and thy sons' sons;

Specially the day that thou stoodest before the LORD thy God in Horeb, when the LORD said unto me, Gather me the people together, and I will make them hear my words, that they may learn to fear me all the days that they shall live upon the earth, and that they may teach their children.

—Deuteronomy 4:9–10

These words, which I command thee this day, shall be in thine heart:

And thou shalt teach them diligently unto thy children, and shalt talk of them when thou sittest in thine house, and when thou walkest by the way, and when thou liest down, and when thou risest up.

And thou shalt bind them for a sign upon thine hand, and they shall be as frontlets between thine eyes.

And thou shalt write them upon the posts of thy house, and on thy gates.

—Deuteronomy 6:6–9

And ye shall teach them your children, speaking of them when thou sittest in thine house, and when thou walkest by the way, when thou liest down, and when thou risest up.

—*Deuteronomy 11:19*

Give ear, O my people, to my law: incline your ears to the words of my mouth.

I will open my mouth in a parable: I will utter dark sayings of old:

Which we have heard and known, and our fathers have told us.

We will not hide them from their children, shewing to the generation to come the praises of the LORD, and his strength, and his wonderful works that he hath done.

For he established a testimony in Jacob, and appointed a law in Israel, which he commanded our fathers, that they should make them known to their children:

That the generation to come might know them, even the children which should be born; who should arise and declare them to their children:

That they might set their hope in God, and not forget the works of God, but keep his commandments:

And might not be as their fathers, a stubborn and rebellious generation; a generation that set not their heart aright, and whose spirit was not stedfast with God.

—*Psalm 78:1–8*

Now his parents went to Jerusalem every year at the feast of the passover.

And when he was twelve years old, they went up to Jerusalem after the custom of the feast.

And when they had fulfilled the days, as they returned, the child Jesus tarried behind in Jerusalem; and Joseph and his mother knew not of it.

But they, supposing him to have been in the company, went a day's journey; and they sought him among their kinsfolk and acquaintance.

And when they found him not, they turned back again to Jerusalem, seeking him.

And it came to pass, that after three days they found him in the temple, sitting in the midst of the doctors, both hearing them, and asking them questions.

And all that heard him were astonished at his understanding and answers.

And when they saw him, they were amazed: and his mother said unto him, Son, why hast thou thus dealt with us? behold, thy father and I have sought thee sorrowing.

And he said unto them, How is it that ye sought me? wist ye not that I must be about my Father's business?

And they understood not the saying which he spake unto them.

—Luke 2:41–50

Provoke not your children to wrath: but bring them up in the nurture and admonition of the Lord.

—Ephesians 6:4b

Help Them Accept Parental Guidance

I put the relation of a fine teacher to a student just below the relation of a mother to a son, and I don't think I could say more than this.

—*Thomas Wolfe*

Forsake not the law of thy mother.

—*Proverbs 1:8b*

Children, obey your parents in all things: for this is well pleasing unto the Lord.

—*Colossians 3:20*

Ye shall fear every man his mother, and his father, and keep my sabbaths: I am the LORD your God.

—*Leviticus 19:3*

My son, if thou wilt receive my words, and hide my commandments with thee;

So that thou incline thine ear unto wisdom, and apply thine heart to understanding;

Yea, if thou criest after knowledge, and liftest up thy voice for understanding;

If thou seekest her as silver, and searchest for her as for hid treasures;

Then shalt thou understand the fear of the LORD, and find the knowledge of God.

—*Proverbs 2:1–5*

He is in the way of life that keepeth instruction: but he that refuseth reproof erreth.

—*Proverbs 10:17*

Whoso despiseth the word shall be destroyed: but he that feareth the commandment shall be rewarded.

—*Proverbs 13:13*

Hear, ye children, the instruction of a father, and attend to know understanding.

For I give you good doctrine, forsake ye not my law.

For I was my father's son, tender and only beloved in the sight of my mother.

He taught me also, and said unto me, Let thine heart retain my words: keep my commandments, and live.

Get wisdom, get understanding: forget it not; neither decline from the words of my mouth.

Forsake her not, and she shall preserve thee: love her, and she shall keep thee.

Wisdom is the principal thing; therefore get wisdom: and with all thy getting get understanding.

Exalt her, and she shall promote thee: she shall bring thee to honour, when thou dost embrace her.

She shall give to thine head an ornament of grace: a crown of glory shall she deliver to thee.

—*Proverbs 4:1–9*

Honour thy father and thy mother, as the LORD thy God hath commanded thee; that thy days may be prolonged, and that it may go well with thee, in the land which the LORD thy God giveth thee.

—*Deuteronomy 5:16*

My son, if thine heart be wise, my heart shall rejoice, even mine.

Yea, my reins shall rejoice, when thy lips speak right things.

Let not thine heart envy sinners: but be thou in the fear of the LORD all the day long.

For surely there is an end; and thine expectation shall not be cut off.

Hear thou, my son, and be wise, and guide thine heart in the way.

Be not among winebibbers; among riotous eaters of flesh:

For the drunkard and the glutton shall come to poverty: and drowsiness shall clothe a man with rags.

Hearken unto thy father that begat thee, and despise not thy mother when she is old.

Buy the truth, and sell it not; also wisdom, and instruction, and understanding.

The father of the righteous shall greatly rejoice: and he that begetteth a wise child shall have joy of him.

Thy father and thy mother shall be glad, and she that bare thee shall rejoice.

My son, give me thine heart, and let thine eyes observe my ways.

—*Proverbs 23:15–26*

Help Them Learn Initiative and Accountability

You cannot plow a field
by turning it over in your mind.

—*Anonymous*

I went by the field of the slothful, and by the vineyard of the man void of understanding;

And, lo, it was all grown over with thorns, and nettles had covered the face thereof, and the stone wall thereof was broken down.

Then I saw, and considered it well: I looked upon it, and received instruction.

Yet a little sleep, a little slumber, a little folding of the hands to sleep:

So shall thy poverty come as one that travelleth; and thy want as an armed man.

—*Proverbs 24:30–34*

Know ye not that they which run in a race run all, but one receiveth the prize? So run, that ye may obtain.

And every man that striveth for the mastery is temperate in all things. Now they do it to obtain a corruptible crown; but we an incorruptible.

I therefore so run, not as uncertainly; so fight I, not as one that beateth the air:

But I keep under my body, and bring it into subjection: lest that by any means, when I have preached to others, I myself should be a castaway.

—1 Corinthians 9:24–27

And that ye study to be quiet, and to do your own business, and to work with your own hands, as we commanded you;

That ye may walk honestly toward them that are without, and that ye may have lack of nothing.

—1 Thessalonians 4:11–12

For even when we were with you, this we commanded you, that if any would not work, neither should he eat.

For we hear that there are some which walk among you disorderly, working not at all, but are busybodies.

Now them that are such we command and exhort by our Lord Jesus Christ, that with quietness they work, and eat their own bread.

—*2 Thessalonians 3:10–12*

Help Them Choose Good Friends

In choosing a friend, go up a step.

—*Jewish proverb*

The righteous is more excellent than his neighbour: but the way of the wicked seduceth them.

—*Proverbs 12:26*

A froward man soweth strife: and a whisperer separateth chief friends.

—*Proverbs 16:28*

He that loveth pureness of heart, for the grace of his lips the king shall be his friend.

—*Proverbs 22:11*

Make no friendship with an angry man;
and with a furious man thou shalt not go.

—*Proverbs 22:24*

Faithful are the wounds of a friend; but the
kisses of an enemy are deceitful.

The full soul loatheth an honeycomb; but
to the hungry soul every bitter thing is sweet.

As a bird that wandereth from her nest, so
is a man that wandereth from his place.

Ointment and perfume rejoice the heart:
so doth the sweetness of a man's friend by
hearty counsel.

Thine own friend, and thy father's friend,
forsake not; neither go into thy brother's
house in the day of thy calamity: for better is
a neighbour that is near than a brother far off.

—*Proverbs 27:6–10*

Help Them Learn to Persevere

*When nothing else seems to help, I go and look
at a stonecutter hammering away at his rock,
perhaps a hundred times without a crack*

showing in it. Yet at the hundred-and-first blow the rock will split in two, and I know that it was not only that blow which split it, but all that had gone before.

—*Jacob A. Riis* [1]

He that loveth pleasure shall be a poor man: he that loveth wine and oil shall not be rich.

—*Proverbs 21:17*

Although the fig tree shall not blossom, neither shall fruit be in the vines; the labour of the olive shall fail, and the fields shall yield no meat; the flock shall be cut off from the fold, and there shall be no herd in the stalls:

Yet I will rejoice in the LORD, I will joy in the God of my salvation.

The LORD God is my strength, and he will make my feet like hinds' feet, and he will make me to walk upon mine high places. To the chief singer on my stringed instruments.

—*Habakkuk 3:17–19*

For the which cause I also suffer these things: nevertheless I am not ashamed: for I know whom I have believed, and am persuaded that he is able to keep that which I have committed unto him against that day.

—2 Timothy 1:12

This know also, that in the last days perilous times shall come.

For men shall be lovers of their own selves, covetous, boasters, proud, blasphemers, disobedient to parents, unthankful, unholy,

Without natural affection, trucebreakers, false accusers, incontinent, fierce, despisers of those that are good,

Traitors, heady, highminded, lovers of pleasures more than lovers of God.

—2 Timothy 3:1–4

Remember: Punishment May Be Required

Punishment is not revenge; it is a means of discipline. It must be used to instill fear of the consequences of criminal acts, in order to protect the law-abiding.

—*Ruth Alexander*

He that spareth his rod hateth his son: but he that loveth him chasteneth him betimes.

—*Proverbs 13:24*

Withhold not correction from the child: for if thou beatest him with the rod, he shall not die.

—*Proverbs 23:13*

Correct thy son, and he shall give thee rest; yea, he shall give delight unto thy soul.

—*Proverbs 29:17*

Be a Merciful and Forgiving Parent— As God Is!

Who is it that loves me—and will love me
forever
with an affection which no chance,
no misery, no crime of mine
can do away?
It is you, my mother.

—*Thomas Carlyle*

Like as a father pitieth his children, so the LORD pitieth them that fear him.

For he knoweth our frame; he remembereth that we are dust.

As for man, his days are as grass: as a flower of the field, so he flourisheth.

For the wind passeth over it, and it is gone; and the place thereof shall know it no more.

But the mercy of the LORD is from everlasting to everlasting upon them that fear him, and his righteousness unto children's children.

—*Psalm 103:13–17*

Bless the LORD, O my soul, and forget not all his benefits:

Who forgiveth all thine iniquities; who healeth all thy diseases;

Who redeemeth thy life from destruction; who crowneth thee with lovingkindness and tender mercies;

Who satisfieth thy mouth with good things; so that thy youth is renewed like the eagle's.

—Psalm 103:2–5

He that covereth his sins shall not prosper: but whoso confesseth and forsaketh them shall have mercy.

—Proverbs 28:13

Therefore will the LORD wait, that he may be gracious unto you, and therefore will he be exalted, that he may have mercy upon you: for the LORD is a God of judgment: blessed are all they that wait for him.

—Isaiah 30:18

It is good for a man that he bear the yoke in his youth.

He sitteth alone and keepeth silence, because he hath borne it upon him.

He putteth his mouth in the dust; if so be there may be hope.

He giveth his cheek to him that smiteth him: he is filled full with reproach.

For the Lord will not cast off for ever:

But though he cause grief, yet will he have compassion according to the multitude of his mercies.

For he doth not afflict willingly nor grieve the children of men.

—Lamentations 3:27–33

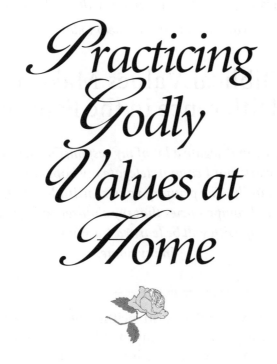

— F o u r —

Practicing Godly Values at Home

How would you describe the values that come through in our culture—especially those conveyed in the entertainment media? Clearly, we as Christian families face a daily barrage of messages and behaviors that fall well below the high standards of our Lord. The kingdom of this world has little in common with His kingdom. Will you turn to Him for help today?

Biblical Values Make a Difference in the Family!

I can delegate a lot of my responsibilities at work, but I cannot delegate my hopes for my family. The primary values, attitudes, skills, and competencies that my children will grow up with will be learned (or not learned) in my home.

—Tim Hansel [1]

Love not the world, neither the things that are in the world. If any man love the world, the love of the Father is not in him.

For all that is in the world, the lust of the flesh, and the lust of the eyes, and the pride of life, is not of the Father, but is of the world.

And the world passeth away, and the lust thereof: but he that doeth the will of God abideth for ever.

—1 John 2:15–17

Be not conformed to this world: but be ye transformed by the renewing of your mind, that ye may prove what is that good, and acceptable, and perfect, will of God.

—*Romans 12:2*

Wherefore gird up the loins of your mind, be sober, and hope to the end for the grace that is to be brought unto you at the revelation of Jesus Christ.

—*1 Peter 1:13*

If ye be reproached for the name of Christ, happy are ye; for the spirit of glory and of God resteth upon you: on their part he is evil spoken of, but on your part he is glorified.

But let none of you suffer as a murderer, or as a thief, or as an evildoer, or as a busybody in other men's matters.

—*1 Peter 4:14–15*

If the world hate you, ye know that it hated me before it hated you.

If ye were of the world, the world would love his own: but because ye are not of the world, but I have chosen you out of the world, therefore the world hateth you.

—John 15:18–19

⋘ *Walk in God's Strength*

O God, thou art my God; early will I seek thee: my soul thirsteth for thee, my flesh longeth for thee in a dry and thirsty land, where no water is.

—Psalm 63:1

For by thee I have run through a troop: by my God have I leaped over a wall.

—2 Samuel 22:30

When thou goest, thy steps shall not be straitened; and when thou runnest, thou shalt not stumble.

—Proverbs 4:12

He giveth power to the faint; and to them that have no might he increaseth strength.

Even the youths shall faint and be weary, and the young men shall utterly fall:

But they that wait upon the LORD shall renew their strength; they shall mount up with wings as eagles; they shall run, and not be weary; and they shall walk, and not faint.

—Isaiah 40:29–31

Ask, and it shall be given you; seek, and ye shall find; knock, and it shall be opened unto you.

—Matthew 7:7

I beseech you therefore, brethren, by the mercies of God, that ye present your bodies a living sacrifice, holy, acceptable unto God, which is your reasonable service.

—Romans 12:1

⋘ *Live by His Spirit*

If ye then, being evil, know how to give good gifts unto your children: how much more shall your heavenly Father give the Holy Spirit to them that ask him?

—Luke 11:13

I will pray the Father, and he shall give you another Comforter, that he may abide with you for ever;

Even the Spirit of truth; whom the world cannot receive, because it seeth him not, neither knoweth him: but ye know him; for he dwelleth with you, and shall be in you.

—John 14:16–17

But the Comforter, which is the Holy Ghost, whom the Father will send in my name, he shall teach you all things, and bring all things to your remembrance, whatsoever I have said unto you.

Peace I leave with you, my peace I give unto you: not as the world giveth, give I unto you. Let not your heart be troubled, neither let it be afraid.

—John 14:26–27

But when the Comforter is come, whom I will send unto you from the Father, even the Spirit of truth, which proceedeth from the Father, he shall testify of me:

—John 15:26

Pursue Values Like These . . .

As the apple is not the cause of the apple tree,
but a fruit of it:
even so good works are not the cause of our
salvation, but a sign and fruit of same.
—Daniel Cawdray

Therefore we ought to give the more earnest heed to the things which we have heard, lest at any time we should let them slip.

For if the word spoken by angels was stedfast, and every transgression and disobedience received a just recompence of reward;

How shall we escape, if we neglect so great salvation?

—Hebrews 2:1–3a

Whatsoever things are true, whatsoever things are honest, whatsoever things are just, whatsoever things are pure, whatsoever things are lovely, whatsoever things are of good report; if there be any virtue, and if there be any praise, think on these things.

—Philippians 4:8

ᐊᐧ Compassion

And I will sow her unto me in the earth; and I will have mercy upon her that had not obtained mercy; and I will say to them which were not my people, Thou art my people; and they shall say, Thou art my God.

—Hosea 2:23

And of some have compassion, making a difference:

And others save with fear, pulling them out of the fire; hating even the garment spotted by the flesh.

—Jude 22–23

ᐊᐧ Gratitude

In every thing give thanks: for this is the will of God in Christ Jesus concerning you.

—1 Thessalonians 5:18

Then went king David in, and sat before the LORD, and he said, Who am I, O Lord GOD? and what is my house, that thou hast brought me hitherto?

And this was yet a small thing in thy sight, O Lord GOD; but thou hast spoken also of thy servant's house for a great while to come. And is this the manner of man, O Lord GOD?

And what can David say more unto thee? for thou, Lord GOD, knowest thy servant.

For thy word's sake, and according to thine own heart, hast thou done all these great things, to make thy servant know them.

Wherefore thou art great, O LORD God: for there is none like thee, neither is there any God beside thee, according to all that we have heard with our ears.

And what one nation in the earth is like thy people, even like Israel, whom God went to redeem for a people to himself, and to make him a name, and to do for you great things and terrible, for thy land, before thy people, which thou redeemedst to thee from Egypt, from the nations and their gods?

For thou hast confirmed to thyself thy people Israel to be a people unto thee for ever: and thou, LORD, art become their God.

And now, O LORD God, the word that thou hast spoken concerning thy servant, and concerning his house, establish it for ever, and do as thou hast said.

And let thy name be magnified for ever, saying, The LORD of hosts is the God over Israel: and let the house of thy servant David be established before thee.

For thou, O LORD of hosts, God of Israel, hast revealed to thy servant, saying, I will build thee an house: therefore hath thy servant found in his heart to pray this prayer unto thee.

And now, O Lord GOD, thou art that God, and thy words be true, and thou hast promised this goodness unto thy servant:

Therefore now let it please thee to bless the house of thy servant, that it may continue for ever before thee: for thou, O Lord GOD, hast spoken it: and with thy blessing let the house of thy servant be blessed for ever.

—*2 Samuel 7:18–29*

And the king turned his face about, and blessed all the congregation of Israel: (and all the congregation of Israel stood;)

And he said, Blessed be the LORD God of Israel, which spake with his mouth unto

David my father, and hath with his hand fulfilled it, saying,

Since the day that I brought forth my people Israel out of Egypt, I chose no city out of all the tribes of Israel to build an house, that my name might be therein; but I chose David to be over my people Israel.

And it was in the heart of David my father to build an house for the name of the LORD God of Israel.

And the LORD said unto David my father, Whereas it was in thine heart to build an house unto my name, thou didst well that it was in thine heart.

Nevertheless thou shalt not build the house; but thy son that shall come forth out of thy loins, he shall build the house unto my name.

And the LORD hath performed his word that he spake, and I am risen up in the room of David my father, and sit on the throne of Israel, as the LORD promised, and have built an house for the name of the LORD God of Israel.

And I have set there a place for the ark, wherein is the covenant of the LORD, which he made with our fathers, when he brought them out of the land of Egypt.

—*1 Kings 8:14–21*

Be careful for nothing; but in every thing by prayer and supplication with thanksgiving let your requests be made known unto God.

—*Philippians 4:6*

⋘ *Faith*

Verily I say unto you, If ye have faith as a grain of mustard seed, ye shall say unto this mountain, Remove hence to yonder place; and it shall remove; and nothing shall be impossible unto you.

—*Matthew 17:20b*

Caleb stilled the people before Moses, and said, Let us go up at once, and possess it; for we are well able to overcome it.

—*Numbers 13:30*

Yea, though I walk through the valley of the shadow of death, I will fear no evil: for thou art with me; thy rod and thy staff they comfort me.

—Psalm 23:4

⋘ *Obedience to God*

Whether therefore ye eat, or drink, or whatsoever ye do, do all to the glory of God.

—1 Corinthians 10:31

And hereby we do know that we know him, if we keep his commandments.

—1 John 2:3

Whosoever believeth that Jesus is the Christ is born of God: and every one that loveth him that begat loveth him also that is begotten of him.

By this we know that we love the children of God, when we love God, and keep his commandments.

For this is the love of God, that we keep his commandments: and his commandments are not grievous.

—1 John 5:1–3

Thou shalt love the LORD thy God with all thine heart, and with all thy soul, and with all thy might.

—*Deuteronomy 6:5*

Let the words of my mouth, and the meditation of my heart, be acceptable in thy sight, O LORD, my strength, and my redeemer.

—*Psalm 19:14*

Blessed are the undefiled in the way, who walk in the law of the LORD.

Blessed are they that keep his testimonies, and that seek him with the whole heart.

They also do no iniquity: they walk in his ways.

Thou hast commanded us to keep thy precepts diligently.

O that my ways were directed to keep thy statutes!

—*Psalm 119:1–5*

No man can serve two masters: for either he will hate the one, and love the other; or else he will hold to the one, and despise the other. Ye cannot serve God and mammon.

—*Matthew 6:24*

And they called them, and commanded them not to speak at all nor teach in the name of Jesus.

But Peter and John answered and said unto them, Whether it be right in the sight of God to hearken unto you more than unto God, judge ye.

For we cannot but speak the things which we have seen and heard.

—Acts 4:18–20

≪ *Hospitality*

He that receiveth a prophet in the name of a prophet shall receive a prophet's reward; and he that receiveth a righteous man in the name of a righteous man shall receive a righteous man's reward.

And whosoever shall give to drink unto one of these little ones a cup of cold water only in the name of a disciple, verily I say unto you, he shall in no wise lose his reward.

—Matthew 10:41–42

Then said he also to him that bade him, When thou makest a dinner or a supper, call not thy friends, nor thy brethren, neither thy kinsmen, nor thy rich neighbours; lest they also bid thee again, and a recompence be made thee.

But when thou makest a feast, call the poor, the maimed, the lame, the blind:

And thou shalt be blessed; for they cannot recompense thee: for thou shalt be recompensed at the resurrection of the just.

—*Luke 14:12–14*

Then Peter went down to the men which were sent unto him from Cornelius; and said, Behold, I am he whom ye seek: what is the cause wherefore ye are come?

And they said, Cornelius the centurion, a just man, and one that feareth God, and of good report among all the nation of the Jews, was warned from God by an holy angel to send for thee into his house, and to hear words of thee.

Then called he them in, and lodged them. And on the morrow Peter went away with them, and certain brethren from Joppa accompanied him.

—*Acts 10:21–23*

And when they were escaped, then they knew that the island was called Melita.

And the barbarous people shewed us no little kindness: for they kindled a fire, and received us every one, because of the present rain, and because of the cold.

—Acts 28:1–2

Beloved, thou doest faithfully whatsoever thou doest to the brethren, and to strangers;

Which have borne witness of thy charity before the church: whom if thou bring forward on their journey after a godly sort, thou shalt do well:

Because that for his name's sake they went forth, taking nothing of the Gentiles.

We therefore ought to receive such, that we might be fellow helpers to the truth.

—3 John 5–8

⋘ *Stewardship*

The earth is the LORD's, and the fulness thereof; the world, and they that dwell therein.

For he hath founded it upon the seas, and established it upon the floods.

—Psalm 24:1–2

What? know ye not that your body is the temple of the Holy Ghost which is in you, which ye have of God, and ye are not your own?

For ye are bought with a price: therefore glorify God in your body, and in your spirit, which are God's.

—*1 Corinthians 6:19–20*

As soon as the commandment came abroad, the children of Israel brought in abundance the firstfruits of corn, wine, and oil, and honey, and of all the increase of the field; and the tithe of all things brought they in abundantly.

And concerning the children of Israel and Judah, that dwelt in the cities of Judah, they also brought in the tithe of oxen and sheep, and the tithe of holy things which were con-secrated unto the LORD their God, and laid them by heaps.

In the third month they began to lay the foundation of the heaps, and finished them in the seventh month.

And when Hezekiah and the princes came and saw the heaps, they blessed the LORD, and his people Israel.

—*2 Chronicles 31:5–8*

For I mean not that other men be eased, and ye burdened:

But by an equality, that now at this time your abundance may be a supply for their want, that their abundance also may be a supply for your want: that there may be equality:

As it is written, He that had gathered much had nothing over; and he that had gathered little had no lack.

—*2 Corinthians 8:13–15*

And when James, Cephas, and John, who seemed to be pillars, perceived the grace that was given unto me, they gave to me and Barnabas the right hands of fellowship; that we should go unto the heathen, and they unto the circumcision.

Only they would that we should remember the poor; the same which I also was forward to do.

Galatians 2:9–10

As every man hath received the gift, even so minister the same one to another, as good stewards of the manifold grace of God.

If any man speak, let him speak as the oracles of God; if any man minister, let him do it as of the ability which God giveth: that God in all things may be glorified through Jesus Christ, to whom be praise and dominion for ever and ever. Amen.

—1 Peter 4:10–11

Pursuing Self-Nurture

Where do you turn when the pressure builds? Whether you're a stay-at-home mom or you work outside the home, you know just how overwhelming your responsibilities can be. There's never enough time—or energy—for all that needs to be done!

The words of Scripture can help: they call you to take care of yourself. God provides everything you need to do it, for He is the ultimate care-giver.

Dealing with Your Stressful Times

Super Moms were faster than a speeding bullet, more powerful than a harsh laxative, and able to leap six shopping carts on double stamp day. . . . She cut the grass, baked her own bread, shoveled the driveway, grew her own herbs, made the children's clothes, altered her husband's suits, played the organ at church, planned the vacation, paid the bills, was on three telephone committees, five car pools, two boards, took her ironing board down every week, stocked the freezer with sides of beef, made her own Christmas cards, voted in every election, saw her dentist twice a year, assisted in the delivery of her dog's puppies, melted down old candles, saved the antifreeze, and had a pencil by her telephone.

—Erma Bombeck [1]

Come unto me, all ye that labour and are heavy laden, and I will give you rest.

Take my yoke upon you, and learn of me; for I am meek and lowly in heart: and ye shall find rest unto your souls.

For my yoke is easy, and my burden is light.

—*Matthew 11:28–30*

Fear thou not; for I am with thee: be not dismayed; for I am thy God: I will strengthen thee; yea, I will help thee; yea, I will uphold thee with the right hand of my righteousness.

—*Isaiah 41:10*

Peace I leave with you, my peace I give unto you: not as the world giveth, give I unto you. Let not your heart be troubled, neither let it be afraid.

—*John 14:27*

If the Son therefore shall make you free, ye shall be free indeed.

—*John 8:36*

Facing Overwhelming Responsibilities?

It is not uncommon for a mother, particularly, to feel overwhelmed by the complexity of her parental assignment. For each child she raises, she is the primary protector of his health, education, intellect, personality, character, and emotional stability. She must serve as physician, nurse, psychologist, teacher, minister, cook, and policeman.

—*James Dobson* [2]

Be careful for nothing; but in every thing by prayer and supplication with thanksgiving let your requests be made known unto God.

And the peace of God, which passeth all understanding, shall keep your hearts and minds through Christ Jesus.

Finally, brethren, whatsoever things are true, whatsoever things are honest, whatsoever things are just, whatsoever things are pure, whatsoever things are lovely, whatsoever things are of good report; if there be any virtue, and if there be any praise, think on these things.

—*Philippians 4:6–8*

For God hath not given us the spirit of fear; but of power, and of love, and of a sound mind.

Be not thou therefore ashamed of the testimony of our Lord, nor of me his prisoner: but be thou partaker of the afflictions of the gospel according to the power of God;

Who hath saved us, and called us with an holy calling, not according to our works, but according to his own purpose and grace, which was given us in Christ Jesus before the world began.

—*2 Timothy 1:7–9*

Maintaining Physical Health

Look to your health; and if you have it, praise
God, and value it next to a good conscience.
For health is the second blessing that we
mortals are capable of—
a blessing that money cannot buy.

—Izaak Walton

I wish above all things that thou mayest
prosper and be in health, even as thy
soul prospereth.

—3 John 2

⋘ *Getting Enough Rest*

Six days thou shalt do thy work, and on the
seventh day thou shalt rest: that thine ox and
thine ass may rest, and the son of thy handmaid, and the stranger, may be refreshed.

—Exodus 23:12

The apostles gathered themselves together unto Jesus, and told him all things, both what they had done, and what they had taught.

And he said unto them, Come ye your-selves apart into a desert place, and rest a while: for there were many coming and going, and they had no leisure so much as to eat.

And they departed into a desert place by ship privately.

—Mark 6:30–32

⋘ *Making Time for Exercise*

For by thee I have run through a troop: by my God have I leaped over a wall.

—2 Samuel 22:30

When thou goest, thy steps shall not be straitened; and when thou runnest, thou shalt not stumble.

—Proverbs 4:12

I beseech you therefore, brethren, by the mercies of God, that ye present your bodies a living sacrifice, holy, acceptable unto God, which is your reasonable service.

—*Romans 12:1*

What? know ye not that your body is the temple of the Holy Ghost which is in you, which ye have of God, and ye are not your own?

For ye are bought with a price: therefore glorify God in your body, and in your spirit, which are God's.

—*1 Corinthians 6:19–20*

For our conversation is in heaven; from whence also we look for the Saviour, the Lord Jesus Christ:

Who shall change our vile body, that it may be fashioned like unto his glorious body, according to the working whereby he is able even to subdue all things unto himself.

—*Philippians 3:20–21*

⋘ *Watching Your Nutrition*

There is nothing better for a man, than that he should eat and drink, and that he should make his soul enjoy good in his labour. This also I saw, that it was from the hand of God.

—*Ecclesiastes 2:24*

And also that every man should eat and drink, and enjoy the good of all his labour, it is the gift of God.

—*Ecclesiastes 3:13*

⋘ *Getting Enough Sleep*

I laid me down and slept; I awaked; for the LORD sustained me.

—*Psalm 3:5*

Stand in awe, and sin not: commune with your own heart upon your bed, and be still. Selah.

—*Psalm 4:4*

When he was entered into a ship, his disciples followed him.

And, behold, there arose a great tempest in the sea, insomuch that the ship was covered with the waves: but he was asleep.

—Matthew 8:23–24

⪻ *Accepting God's Peace*

For in the time of trouble he shall hide me in his pavilion: in the secret of his tabernacle shall he hide me; he shall set me up upon a rock.

—Psalm 27:5

Blessed are the poor in spirit: for theirs is the kingdom of heaven.

Blessed are they that mourn: for they shall be comforted.

Blessed are the meek: for they shall inherit the earth.

Blessed are they which do hunger and thirst after righteousness: for they shall be filled.

Blessed are the merciful: for they shall obtain mercy.

Blessed are the pure in heart: for they shall see God.

Blessed are the peacemakers: for they shall be called the children of God.

Blessed are they which are persecuted for righteousness' sake: for theirs is the kingdom of heaven.

Blessed are ye, when men shall revile you, and persecute you, and shall say all manner of evil against you falsely, for my sake.

Rejoice, and be exceeding glad: for great is your reward in heaven: for so persecuted they the prophets which were before you.

—Matthew 5:3–12

Staying Emotionally Healthy

In spite of illness, in spite even of the archenemy sorrow, one can remain alive long past the usual date of disintegration if one is unafraid of change, insatiable in intellectual curiosity, interested in big things, and happy in small ways.

—*Edith Warton* [3]

⋘ *Are You Open to Self-Examination?*

No man, when he hath lighted a candle, putteth it in a secret place, neither under a bushel, but on a candlestick, that they which come in may see the light.

The light of the body is the eye: therefore when thine eye is single, thy whole body also is full of light; but when thine eye is evil, thy body also is full of darkness.

Take heed therefore that the light which is in thee be not darkness.

If thy whole body therefore be full of light, having no part dark, the whole shall be full of light, as when the bright shining of a candle doth give thee light.

—*Luke 11:33–36*

For there is nothing covered, that shall not be revealed; neither hid, that shall not be known.

Therefore whatsoever ye have spoken in darkness shall be heard in the light; and that which ye have spoken in the ear in closets shall be proclaimed upon the housetops.

—*Luke 12:2–3*

For we dare not make ourselves of the numbers or compare ourselves with some that commend themselves: but they measuring themselves by themselves, and comparing themselves among themselves, are not wise.

—*2 Corinthians 10:12*

⫷ Are You Enslaved to Bad Habits?

For mine iniquities are gone over mine head: as an heavy burden they are too heavy for me.

My wounds stink and are corrupt because of my foolishness.

I am troubled; I am bowed down greatly; I go mourning all the day long.

For my loins are filled with a loathsome disease: and there is no soundness in my flesh.

I am feeble and sore broken: I have roared by reason of the disquietness of my heart.

—*Psalm 38:4–8*

When I thought to know this, it was too painful for me.

—*Psalm 73:16*

Why is my pain perpetual, and my wound incurable, which refuseth to be healed? wilt thou be altogether unto me as a liar, and as waters that fail?

—*Jeremiah 15:18*

Who can understand his errors? cleanse thou me from secret faults.

Keep back thy servant also from presumptuous sins; let them not have dominion over me: then shall I be upright, and I shall be innocent from the great transgression.

Let the words of my mouth, and the meditation of my heart, be acceptable in thy sight, O LORD, my strength, and my redeemer.

—*Psalm 19:12–14*

If thy right eye offend thee, pluck it out, and cast it from thee: for it is profitable for thee that one of thy members should perish, and not that thy whole body should be cast into hell.

And if thy right hand offend thee, cut if off, and cast it from thee: for it is profitable for thee that one of thy members should perish, and not that thy whole body should be cast into hell.

—*Matthew 5:29–30*

Finding Meaning and Purpose in the Lord

God, who has made us, knows what we are and that our happiness lies in him. Yet we will not seek it in him as long as he leaves us any other resort where it can even plausibly be looked for. While what we call "our own life" remains agreeable we will not surrender it to him.

—C. S. Lewis[4]

I said in mine heart concerning the estate of the sons of men, that God might manifest them, and that they might see that they themselves are beasts.

For that which befalleth the sons of men befalleth beasts; even one thing befalleth them: as the one dieth, so dieth the other; yea, they have all one breath; so that a man hath no preeminence above a beast: for all is vanity.

All go unto one place; all are of the dust, and all turn to dust again.

—*Ecclesiastes 3:18–20*

Recognizing How Loved You Are!

The greatest happiness of life is the conviction
that we are loved—loved for ourselves,
or rather, loved in spite of ourselves.

—*Victor Hugo*

⋘ *So Wonderfully Made!*

I will praise thee; for I am fearfully and wonderfully made: marvellous are thy works; and that my soul knoweth right well.

My substance was not hid from thee, when I was made in secret, and curiously wrought in the lowest parts of the earth.

Thine eyes did see my substance, yet being unperfect; and in thy book all my members were written, which in continuance were fashioned, when as yet there was none of them.

—*Psalm 139:14–16*

❦ *Esteemed by God!*

O LORD our Lord, how excellent is thy name in all the earth! who hast set thy glory above the heavens.

Out of the mouth of babes and sucklings hast thou ordained strength because of thine enemies, that thou mightest still the enemy and the avenger.

When I consider thy heavens, the work of thy fingers, the moon and the stars, which thou hast ordained;

What is man, that thou art mindful of him? and the son of man, that thou visitest him?

For thou hast made him a little lower than the angels, and hast crowned him with glory and honour.

Thou madest him to have dominion over the works of thy hands; thou hast put all things under his feet:

All sheep and oxen, yea, and the beasts of the field;

The fowl of the air, and the fish of the sea, and whatsoever passeth through the paths of the seas.

O LORD our Lord, how excellent is thy name in all the earth!

—Psalm 8:1–9

Letting God Nurture You

My God, I choose the whole lot. No point in becoming a saint by halves. I'm not afraid of suffering for your sake; the only thing I'm afraid of is clinging to my own will. Take it. I want the whole lot, everything whatsoever that is your will for me.

—Therese of Lisieux

In the multitude of my thoughts within me thy comforts delight my soul.

—Psalm 94:19

For he maketh sore, and bindeth up: he woundeth, and his hands make whole.

—Job 5:18

Praise ye the LORD: for it is good to sing praises unto our God; for it is pleasant; and praise is comely.

The LORD doth build up Jerusalem: he gathereth together the outcasts of Israel.

He healeth the broken in heart, and bindeth up their wounds.

—Psalm 147:1–3

Therefore all they that devour thee shall be devoured; and all thine adversaries, every one of them, shall go into captivity; and they that spoil thee shall be a spoil, and all that prey upon thee will I give for a prey.

For I will restore health unto thee, and I will heal thee of thy wounds, saith the LORD; because they called thee an Outcast, saying, This is Zion, whom no man seeketh after.

—*Jeremiah 30:16–17*

Keeping the Romance Alive

Someone has said that the best thing we can do for our children is to stay deeply in love with our spouse. Of course, that is one of the best things we can do for ourselves, too! What could you do—this very day—to keep the flames of affection glowing warm and bright?

God Made Marriage

Eternal God, author of harmony
and happiness,
we thank you for the gift of marriage
in which men and women may seek and find
the consummation of bodily union,
the satisfaction of life-long companionship,
and the fulfillment of creative and
responsible parenthood.
Give patience to those who look forward
to marriage;
give courage to those who face trials within
their marriage;
give comfort to those whose marriage
has broken;
And to those whose marriages are successful
and fruitful
give gratitude and understanding,
that they may be examples to all of your
great love.
Through Jesus our Lord.

—Michael Saward [1]

So God created man in his own image, in the image of God created he him; male and female created he them.

—*Genesis 1:27*

The LORD God said, It is not good that the man should be alone; I will make him an help meet for him.

And out of the ground the LORD God formed every beast of the field, and every fowl of the air; and brought them unto Adam to see what he would call them: and whatsoever Adam called every living creature, that was the name thereof.

And Adam gave names to all cattle, and to the fowl of the air, and to every beast of the field; but for Adam there was not found an help meet for him.

And the LORD God caused a deep sleep to fall upon Adam and he slept: and he took one of his ribs, and closed up the flesh instead thereof;

And the rib, which the LORD God had taken from man, made he a woman, and brought her unto the man.

And Adam said, This is now bone of my bones, and flesh of my flesh: she shall be called Woman, because she was taken out of Man.

Therefore shall a man leave his father and his mother, and shall cleave unto his wife: and they shall be one flesh.

And they were both naked, the man and his wife, and were not ashamed.

—Genesis 2:18–25

Marriage is honourable in all, and the bed undefiled.

—Hebrews 13:4a

When a man hath taken a new wife, he shall not go out to war, neither shall he be charged with any business: but he shall be free at home one year, and shall cheer up his wife which he hath taken.

—Deuteronomy 24:5

So Keep the Romance Alive!

[Yet] a love which depends solely on romance, on the combustion of two attracting chemistries, tends to fizzle out. The famous lovers usually end up dead. A long-term marriage has to move beyond chemistry to compatibility, to friendship, to companionship. It is certainly not that passion disappears, but that it is conjoined with other ways of love.

—*Madeleine L'Engle*[2]

My beloved is white and ruddy, the chiefest among ten thousand.

His head is as the most fine gold, his locks are bushy, and black as a raven.

His eyes are as the eyes of doves by the rivers of waters, washed with milk, and fitly set.

His cheeks are as a bed of spices, as sweet flowers: his lips like lilies, dropping sweet smelling myrrh.

His hands are as gold rings set with the beryl: his belly is as bright ivory overlaid with sapphires.

His legs are as pillars of marble, set upon sockets of fine gold: his countenance is as Lebanon, excellent as the cedars.

His mouth is most sweet: yea, he is altogether lovely. This is my beloved, and this is my friend, O daughters of Jerusalem.

—Song of Solomon 5:10–16

Make haste, my beloved, and be thou like to a roe or to a young hart upon the mountains of spices.

—Song of Solomon 8:14

Moreover the word of the LORD came to me, saying,

Go and cry in the ears of Jerusalem, saying, Thus saith the LORD; I remember thee, the kindness of thy youth, the love of thine espousals, when thou wentest after me in the wilderness, in a land that was not sown.

Israel was holiness unto the LORD, and the firstfruits of his increase: all that devour him shall offend; evil shall come upon them, saith the LORD.

—Jeremiah 2:1–3

And unto the married I command, yet not I, but the Lord, Let not the wife depart from her husband:

But and if she depart, let her remain unmarried, or be reconciled to her husband: and let not the husband put away his wife.

But to the rest speak I, not the Lord: If any brother hath a wife that believeth not, and she be pleased to dwell with him, let him not put her away.

And the woman which hath an husband that believeth not, and if he be pleased to dwell with her, let her not leave him.

For the unbelieving husband is sanctified by the wife, and the unbelieving wife is sanctified by the husband: else were your children unclean; but now are they holy.

But if the unbelieving depart, let him depart. A brother or a sister is not under bondage in such cases: but God hath called us to peace.

For what knowest thou, O wife, whether thou shalt save thy husband? or how knowest thou, O man, whether thou shalt save thy wife?

—*1 Corinthians 7:10–16*

Commit to Sexual Faithfulness

The monstrosity of sexual intercourse outside marriage is that those who indulge in it are trying to isolate one kind of union (the sexual) from all the other kinds of union which were intended to go along with it and make up the total union. The Christian attitude does not mean there's anything wrong about sexual pleasure, any more than about the pleasure of eating. It means that you must not isolate that pleasure and try to get it by itself, any more than you ought to try to get the pleasures of taste without swallowing and digesting, by chewing things and spitting them out again.

—C. S. Lewis[3]

I made a covenant with mine eyes; why then should I think upon a maid?

For what portion of God is there from above? and what inheritance of the Almighty from on high?

Is not destruction to the wicked? and a strange punishment to the workers of iniquity?

Doth not he see my ways, and count all my steps?

If I have walked with vanity, or if my foot hath hasted to deceit;

Let me be weighed in an even balance, that God may know mine integrity.

If my step hath turned out of the way, and mine heart walked after mine eyes, and if any blot hath cleaved to mine hands;

Then let me sow, and let another eat; yea, let my offspring be rooted out.

If mine heart have been deceived by a woman, or if I have laid wait at my neighbour's door;

Then let my wife grind unto another, and let others bow down upon her.

For this is an heinous crime; yea, it is an iniquity to be punished by the judges.

For it is a fire that consumeth to destruction, and would root out all mine increase.

—Job 31:1–12

When wisdom entereth into thine heart, and knowledge is pleasant unto thy soul;

Discretion shall preserve thee, understanding shall keep thee:

To deliver thee from the way of the evil man, from the man that speaketh froward things;

Who leave the paths of uprightness, to walk in the ways of darkness;

Who rejoice to do evil, and delight in the frowardness of the wicked;

Whose ways are crooked, and they froward in their paths:

To deliver thee from the strange woman, even from the stranger which flattereth with her words;

Which forsaketh the guide of her youth, and forgetteth the covenant of her God.

For her house inclineth unto death, and her paths unto the dead.

None that go unto her return again, neither take they hold of the paths of life.

That thou mayest walk in the way of good men, and keep the paths of the righteous.

—*Proverbs 2:10–20*

Live joyfully with the wife whom thou lovest all the days of the life of thy vanity, which he hath given thee under the sun, all the days of thy vanity: for that is thy portion in this life, and in thy labour which thou takest under the sun.

—Ecclesiastes 9:9

Ye have heard that it was said by them of old time, Thou shalt not commit adultery:

But I say unto you, That whosoever looketh on a woman to lust after her hath committed adultery with her already in his heart.

—Matthew 5:27–28

Likewise reckon ye also yourselves to be dead indeed unto sin, but alive unto God through Jesus Christ our Lord.

Let not sin therefore reign in your mortal body, that ye should obey it in the lusts thereof.

Neither yield ye your members as instruments of unrighteousness unto sin: but yield yourselves unto God, as those that are alive from the dead, and your members as instruments of righteousness unto God.

For sin shall not have dominion over you: for ye are not under the law, but under grace.

—*Romans 6:11–14*

Meats for the belly, and the belly for meats: but God shall destroy both it and them. Now the body is not for fornication, but for the Lord; and the Lord for the body.

And God hath both raised up the Lord, and will also raise up us by his own power.

Know ye not that your bodies are the members of Christ? shall I then take the members of Christ, and make them the members of an harlot? God forbid.

—*1 Corinthians 6:13–15*

There hath no temptation taken you but such as is common to man: but God is faithful, who will not suffer you to be tempted above that ye are able; but will with the temptation also make a way to escape, that ye may be able to bear it.

—*1 Corinthians 10:13*

For this is the will of God, even your sanctification, that ye should abstain from fornication:

That every one of you should know how to possess his vessel in sanctification and honour;

Not in the lust of concupiscence, even as the Gentiles which know not God:

That no man go beyond and defraud his brother in any matter: because that the Lord is the avenger of all such, as we also have fore-warned you and testified.

For God hath not called us unto uncleanness, but unto holiness.

He therefore that despiseth, despiseth not man, but God, who hath also given unto us his holy Spirit.

—*1 Thessalonians 4:3–8*

Flee also youthful lusts: but follow righteousness, faith, charity, peace, with them that call on the Lord out of a pure heart.

—*2 Timothy 2:22*

Dearly beloved, I beseech you as strangers and pilgrims, abstain from fleshly lusts, which war against the soul.

—*1 Peter 2:11*

Make Your Marriage the Best It Can Be

Chains do not hold a marriage together. It is threads, hundreds of tiny threads that sew people together through the years.

—*Simone Signoret*

Let thy fountain be blessed: and rejoice with the wife of thy youth.

Let her be as the loving hind and pleasant roe; let her breasts satisfy thee at all times; and be thou ravished always with her love.

And why wilt thou, my son, be ravished with a strange woman, and embrace the bosom of a stranger?

—*Proverbs 5:18–20*

House and riches are the inheritance of fathers: and a prudent wife is from the LORD.

—*Proverbs 19:14*

Then will I cause to cease from the cities of Judah, and from the streets of Jerusalem, the voice of mirth, and the voice of gladness, the voice of the bridegroom, and the voice of the bride: for the land shall be desolate.

—Jeremiah 7:34

⋙ *With Mutual Honesty*

That we henceforth be no more children, tossed to and fro, and carried about with every wind of doctrine, by the sleight of men, and cunning craftiness, whereby they lie in wait to deceive;

But speaking the truth in love, may grow up into him in all things, which is the head, even Christ.

—Ephesians 4:14–15

Wherefore, Job, I pray thee, hear my speeches, and hearken to all my words.

Behold, now I have opened my mouth, my tongue hath spoken in my mouth.

My words shall be of the uprightness of my heart: and my lips shall utter knowledge clearly.

The spirit of God hath made me, and the breath of the Almighty hath given me life.

If thou canst answer me, set thy words in order before me, stand up.

—Job 33:1–5

Who shall ascend into the hill of the LORD? or who shall stand in his holy place?

He that hath clean hands, and a pure heart; who hath not lifted up his soul unto vanity, nor sworn deceitfully.

—Psalm 24:3–4

Two things have I required of thee; deny me them not before I die:

Remove far from me vanity and lies: give me neither poverty nor riches; feed me with food convenient for me:

Lest I be full, and deny thee, and say, Who is the LORD? or lest I be poor, and steal, and take the name of my God in vain.

—Proverbs 30:7–9

Then came also publicans to be baptized, and said unto him, Master, what shall we do?

And he said unto them, Exact no more than that which is appointed you.

—Luke 3:12–13

☙ *With Constant Thoughtfulness*

Bear ye one another's burdens, and so fulfil the law of Christ.

For if a man think himself to be something, when he is nothing, he deceiveth himself.

But let every man prove his own work, and then shall he have rejoicing in himself alone, and not in another.

—*Galatians 6:2–4*

With all lowliness and meekness, with longsuffering, forbearing one another in love;

Endeavouring to keep the unity of the Spirit in the bond of peace.

—*Ephesians 4:2–3*

Then Jesus six days before the passover came to Bethany, where Lazarus was which had been dead, whom he raised from the dead.

There they made him a supper; and Martha served: but Lazarus was one of them that sat at the table with him.

Then took Mary a pound of ointment of spikenard, very costly, and anointed the feet of Jesus, and wiped his feet with her hair: and the house was filled with the odour of the ointment.

Then saith one of his disciples, Judas Iscariot, Simon's son, which should betray him,

Why was not this ointment sold for three hundred pence, and given to the poor?

This he said, not that he cared for the poor; but because he was a thief, and had the bag, and bare what was put therein.

Then said Jesus, Let her alone: against the day of my burying hath she kept this.

—John 12:1–7

With Loving Communication

But speaking the truth in love, may grow up into him in all things, which is the head, even Christ:

From whom the whole body fitly joined together and compacted by that which every joint supplieth, according to the effectual working in the measure of every part, maketh increase of the body unto the edifying of itself in love.

—Ephesians 4:15–16

Speaking to yourselves in psalms and hymns and spiritual songs, singing and making melody in your heart to the Lord;

Giving thanks always for all things unto God and the Father in the name of our Lord Jesus Christ.

—Ephesians 5:19–20

Finding Encouragement in Tough Times

You already know that being a parent can be the most rewarding experience imaginable. But no one ever said it would be easy. Discouragement is always just around the corner, because progress in ourselves and in our families can be slow, spiritual growth a matter of fits and starts. Yet, with God's spirit working within us, we're always on the upward trail. And His promises can encourage us when the going gets tough.

Rely on the Sufficiency of Christ . . .
Lord, we are rivers running to thy sea,
Our waves and ripples all derived from thee:
A nothing we should have, a nothing be,
Except for thee.
Sweet are the waters of thy shoreless sea,
Make sweet our waters that make haste
to thee;
Pour in they sweetness, that ourselves may be
Sweetness to thee.

—*Christina Rossetti*[1]

The LORD is my shepherd; I shall not want.

He maketh me to lie down in green pastures: he leadeth me beside the still waters.

He restoreth my soul: he leadeth me in the paths of righteousness for his name's sake.

Yea, though I walk through the valley of the shadow of death, I will fear no evil: for thou art with me; thy rod and thy staff they comfort me.

—*Psalm 23:1–4*

Such trust have we through Christ to God-ward:

Not that we are sufficient of ourselves to think any thing as of ourselves; but our sufficiency is of God.

—2 Corinthians 3:4–5

My help cometh from the LORD, which made heaven and earth.

He will not suffer thy foot to be moved: he that keepeth thee will not slumber.

—Psalm 121:2–3

In the beginning was the Word, and the Word was with God, and the Word was God.

The same was in the beginning with God.

All things were made by him; and without him was not any thing made that was made.

In him was life; and the life was the light of men.

—John 1:1–4

For though I would desire to glory, I shall not be a fool; for I will say the truth: but now I forbear, lest any man should think of me above that which he seeth me to be, or that he heareth of me.

And lest I should be exalted above measure through the abundance of the revelations, there was given to me a thorn in the flesh, the messenger of Satan to buffet me, lest I should be exalted above measure.

For this thing I besought the Lord thrice, that it might depart from me.

And he said unto me, My grace is sufficient for thee: for my strength is made perfect in weakness. Most gladly therefore will I rather glory in my infirmities, that the power of Christ may rest upon me.

Therefore I take pleasure in infirmities, in reproaches, in necessities, in persecutions, in distresses for Christ's sake: for when I am weak, then am I strong.

—*2 Corinthians 12:6–10*

I can do all things through Christ which strengtheneth me.

—*Philippians 4:13*

⫷ *When You Feel Ashamed . . .*

My confusion is continually before me,
and the shame of my face hath covered me.

—Psalm 44:15

I sought the LORD, and he heard me, and
delivered me from all my fears.

They looked unto him, and were lightened:
and their faces were not ashamed.

—Psalm 34:4–5

Thou hast known my reproach, and my
shame, and my dishonour: mine adversaries
are all before thee.

—Psalm 69:19

Fear not; for thou shalt not be ashamed:
neither be thou confounded; for thou shalt
not be put to shame: for thou shalt forget the
shame of thy youth, and shalt not remember
the reproach of thy widowhood any more.

—Isaiah 54:4

For your shame ye shall have double; and for confusion they shall rejoice in their portion: therefore in their land they shall possess the double: everlasting joy shall be unto them.

—Isaiah 61:7

As it is written, Behold, I lay in Sion a stumblingstone and rock of offence: and whosoever believeth on him shall not be ashamed.

—Romans 9:33

⋘ When You Feel Tempted . . .

The LORD shall preserve thee from all evil: he shall preserve thy soul.

The LORD shall preserve thy going out and thy coming in from this time forth, and even for evermore.

—Psalm 121:7–8

Rejoice not against me, O mine enemy: when I fall, I shall arise; when I sit in darkness, the LORD shall be a light unto me.

—Micah 7:8

For the weapons of our warfare are not carnal, but mighty through God to the pulling down of strongholds.

—2 Corinthians 10:4

But the Lord is faithful, who shall stablish you, and keep you from evil.

—2 Thessalonians 3:3

And the Lord shall deliver me from every evil work, and will preserve me unto his heavenly kingdom: to whom be glory for ever and ever. Amen.

—2 Timothy 4:18

The Lord knoweth how to deliver the godly out of temptations, and to reserve the unjust unto the day of judgment to be punished.

—2 Peter 2:9

⋘ *When You Feel Depressed . . .*

When I would comfort myself against sorrow, my heart is faint in me.

—Jeremiah 8:18

And it shall be, when they say unto thee, Wherefore sighest thou? that thou shalt answer, For the tidings; because it cometh: and every heart shall melt, and all hands shall be feeble, and every spirit shall faint, and all knees shall be weak as water: behold, it cometh, and shall be brought to pass, saith the Lord GOD.

—*Ezekiel 21:7*

When my soul fainted within me I remembered the LORD: and my prayer came in unto thee, into thine holy temple.

—*Jonah 2:7*

For this thing I besought the Lord thrice, that it might depart from me.

And he said unto me, My grace is sufficient for thee: for my strength is made perfect in weakness. Most gladly therefore will I rather glory in my infirmities, that the power of Christ may rest upon me. . . .

For though he was crucified through weakness, yet he liveth by the power of God. For we also are weak in him, but we shall live with him by the power of God toward you.

—*2 Corinthians 12:8–9; 13:4*

Finally, my brethren, be strong in the Lord, and in the power of his might.

—Ephesians 6:10

≪ *When You're Afraid . . .*

Fear came upon me, and trembling, which made all my bones to shake.

—Job 4:14

Be strong and of a good courage, fear not, nor be afraid of them: for the LORD thy God, he it is that doth go with thee; he will not fail thee, nor forsake thee.

—Deuteronomy 31:6

Have not I commanded thee? Be strong and of a good courage; be not afraid, neither be thou dismayed: for the LORD thy God is with thee whithersoever thou goest.

—Joshua 1:9

The LORD is my light and my salvation; whom shall I fear? the LORD is the strength of my life; of whom shall I be afraid?

When the wicked, even mine enemies and my foes, came upon me to eat up my flesh, they stumbled and fell.

Though an host should encamp against me, my heart shall not fear: though war should rise against me, in this will I be confident.

—Psalm 27:1–3

For I have heard the slander of many: fear was on every side: while they took counsel together against me, they devised to take away my life.

—Psalm 31:13

Therefore will not we fear, though the earth be removed, and though the mountains be carried into the midst of the sea.

—Psalm 46:2

Hearken unto me, ye that know righteousness, the people in whose heart is my law; fear ye not the reproach of men, neither be ye afraid of their revilings.

—*Isaiah 51:7*

There is no fear in love; but perfect love casteth out fear: because fear hath torment. He that feareth is not made perfect in love.

—*1 John 4:18*

⋘ *When You Are Suffering . . .*

We are troubled on every side, yet not distressed; we are perplexed, but not in despair;

Persecuted, but not forsaken; cast down, but not destroyed;

Always bearing about in the body the dying of the Lord Jesus, that the life also of Jesus might be made manifest in our body. . . .

For our light affliction, which is but for a moment, worketh for us a far more exceeding and eternal weight of glory;

While we look not at the things which are seen, but at the things which are not seen: for the things which are seen are temporal; but the things which are not seen are eternal.

—*2 Corinthians 4:8–10, 17–18*

And if children, then heirs; heirs of God, and joint-heirs with Christ; if so be that we suffer with him, that we may be also glorified together.

For I reckon that the sufferings of this present time are not worthy to be compared with the glory which shall be revealed in us.

—*Romans 8:17–18*

Thou therefore endure hardness, as a good soldier of Jesus Christ. . . .

It is a faithful saying: For if we be dead with him, we shall also live with him:

If we suffer, we shall also reign with him: if we deny him, he also will deny us.

—*2 Timothy 2:3, 11–12*

But the God of all grace, who hath called us unto his eternal glory by Christ Jesus, after that ye have suffered a while, make you perfect, stablish, strengthen, settle you.

To him be glory and dominion for ever and ever. Amen.

—*1 Peter 5:10–11*

✦ When You're Angry. . .

Be ye angry, and sin not: let not the sun go down upon your wrath.

—*Ephesians 4:26*

Stand in awe, and sin not: commune with your own heart upon your bed, and be still. Selah.

—*Psalm 4:4*

But I say unto you, That whosoever is angry with his brother without a cause shall be in danger of the judgment: and whosoever shall say to his brother, Raca, shall be in danger of the council: but whosoever shall say, Thou fool, shall be in danger of hell fire.

—*Matthew 5:22*

✦ When You Struggle with Bitterness . . .

My soul is weary of my life; I will leave my complaint upon myself; I will speak in the bitterness of my soul.

—*Job 10:1*

Thou hast neither part nor lot in this matter:
for thy heart is not right in the sight of God.

Repent therefore of this thy wickedness,
and pray God, if perhaps the thought of thine
heart may be forgiven thee.

For I perceive that thou art in the gall of
bitterness, and in the bond of iniquity.

—*Acts 8:21–23*

Let all bitterness, and wrath, and anger,
and clamour, and evil speaking, be put away
from you, with all malice.

—*Ephesians 4:31*

Looking diligently lest any man fail of the
grace of God; lest any root of bitterness
springing up trouble you, and thereby many
be defiled.

—*Hebrews 12:15*

Receive Encouragement from the Wounds of Christ

The wounds of Christ were the greatest outlets of His glory that ever were. The divine glory shone more out of His wounds than out of all His life before. The veil was then rent in twain, and the full heart of God allowed to stream through. It was a human body that writhed, pale and racked, upon the accursed tree; they were human hands that were pierced so rudely by the nails; it was human blood that streamed from hands, and feet, and side; the eye that meekly turned to His Father was a human eye; the soul that yearned over His mother was a human soul. But oh, there was divine glory streaming through all! Every wound was a fount to speak of the grace and love of God!

—Robert Murray M'Cheyne[2]

⋘ *Light of the World*

Then spake Jesus again unto them, saying, I am the light of the world: he that followeth me shall not walk in darkness, but shall have the light of life.

—John 8:12

I must work the works of him that sent me, while it is day: the night cometh, when no man can work.

As long as I am in the world, I am the light of the world.

—John 9:4–5

⋘ *The Door for the Sheep*

Then said Jesus unto them again, Verily, verily, I say unto you, I am the door of the sheep.

All that ever came before me are thieves and robbers: but the sheep did not hear them.

I am the door: by me if any man enter in, he shall be saved, and shall go in and out, and find pasture.

The thief cometh not, but for to steal, and to kill, and to destroy: I am come that they

might have life, and that they might have it
more abundantly.

⋘ *The Good Shepherd*

I am the good shepherd: the good shepherd
giveth his life for the sheep.

But he that is an hireling, and not the shepherd, whose own the sheep are not, seeth the
wolf coming, and leaveth the sheep, and
fleeth: and the wolf catcheth them, and scat-
tereth the sheep.

The hireling fleeth, because he is an hireling, and careth not for the sheep.

I am the good shepherd, and know my
sheep, and am known of mine.

As the Father knoweth me, even so know I
the Father: and I lay down my life for the sheep.

And other sheep I have, which are not of
this fold: them also I must bring, and they
shall hear my voice; and there shall be one
fold, and one shepherd.

Therefore doth my Father love me, because
I lay down my life, that I might take it again.

No man taketh it from me, but I lay it down of myself. I have power to lay it down, and I have power to take it again. This commandment have I received of my Father.

—John 10:11–18

⋘ *The Resurrection and the Life*

Then said Martha unto Jesus, Lord, if thou hadst been here, my brother had not died.

But I know, that even now, whatsoever thou wilt ask of God, God will give it thee.

Jesus saith unto her, Thy brother shall rise again.

Martha saith unto him, I know that he shall rise again in the resurrection at the last day.

Jesus said unto her, I am the resurrection, and the life: he that believeth in me, though he were dead, yet shall he live:

And whosoever liveth and believeth in me shall never die. Believest thou this?

—John 11:21–26

⟨⟨⟨ *The Bread of Life*

Jesus said unto them, I am the bread of life: he that cometh to me shall never hunger; and he that believeth on me shall never thirst.

But I said unto you, That ye also have seen me, and believe not.

All that the Father giveth me shall come to me; and him that cometh to me I will in no wise cast out.

For I came down from heaven, not to do mine own will, but the will of him that sent me.

And this is the Father's will which hath sent me, that of all which he hath given me I should lose nothing, but should raise it up again at the last day.

And this is the will of him that sent me, that every one which seeth the Son, and believeth on him, may have everlasting life: and I will raise him up at the last day.

—John 6:35–40

Biblical Mothers to Follow

So, we have no heroes anymore?

Perhaps it's time to look into the Scriptures! There we find plenty of heroic women who have stood the test of time—providing the best of spiritual examples to emulate. Who is your personal favorite? What might you do today to mirror her admirable character?

A Great Role Model . . .

Grace was in all her steps, heaven in her eye.
In every gesture dignity and love.

—*John Milton*

Who can find a virtuous woman? for her price is far above rubies.

The heart of her husband doth safely trust in her, so that he shall have no need of spoil.

She will do him good and not evil all the days of her life.

She seeketh wool, and flax, and worketh willingly with her hands.

She is like the merchants' ships; she bringeth her food from afar.

She riseth also while it is yet night, and giveth meat to her household, and a portion to her maidens.

She considereth a field, and buyeth it: with the fruit of her hands she planteth a vineyard.

She girdeth her loins with strength, and strengtheneth her arms.

She perceiveth that her merchandise is good: her candle goeth not out by night.

She layeth her hands to the spindle, and her hands hold the distaff.

She stretcheth out her hand to the poor; yea, she reacheth forth her hands to the needy.

She is not afraid of the snow for her household: for all her household are clothed with scarlet.

She maketh herself coverings of tapestry; her clothing is silk and purple.

Her husband is known in the gates, when he sitteth among the elders of the land.

She maketh fine linen, and selleth it; and delivereth girdles unto the merchant.

Strength and honour are her clothing; and she shall rejoice in time to come.

She openeth her mouth with wisdom; and in her tongue is the law of kindness.

She looketh well to the ways of her household, and eateth not the bread of idleness.

Her children arise up, and call her blessed; her husband also, and he praiseth her.

Many daughters have done virtuously, but thou excellest them all.

Favour is deceitful, and beauty is vain: but a woman that feareth the LORD, she shall be praised.

Give her of the fruit of her hands; and let her own works praise her in the gates.

—*Proverbs 31:10–31*

Others to Emulate, Too . . .

Above all, she was a woman of deep inner resources: her certainties were unnerving; the dreams by which she saw the course of her son's life were impressive, and she was confident she could tell, instinctively, which of these dreams were authentic.

—Peter Brown, describing Monica, Augustine's Mother [1]

⋘ Moses' Mother

There went a man of the house of Levi, and took to wife a daughter of Levi.

And the woman conceived, and bare a son: and when she saw him that he was a goodly child, she hid him three months.

And when she could not longer hide him, she took for him an ark of bulrushes, and daubed it with slime and with pitch, and put the child therein; and she laid it in the flags by the river's brink.

And his sister stood afar off, to wit what would be done to him.

And the daughter of Pharaoh came down to wash herself at the river; and her maidens walked along by the river's side; and when she saw the ark among the flags, she sent her maid to fetch it.

And when she had opened it, she saw the child: and, behold, the babe wept. And she had compassion on him, and said, This is one of the Hebrews' children.

Then said his sister to Pharaoh's daughter, Shall I go and call to thee a nurse of the Hebrew women, that she may nurse the child for thee?

And Pharaoh's daughter said to her, Go. And the maid went and called the child's mother.

And Pharaoh's daughter said unto her, Take this child away, and nurse it for me, and I will give thee thy wages. And the woman took the child, and nursed it.

And the child grew, and she brought him unto Pharaoh's daughter, and he became her son. And she called his name Moses: and she said, Because I drew him out of the water.

—*Exodus 2:1–10*

⪻ *Elizabeth: John the Baptist's Mother*

After those days his wife Elisabeth conceived, and hid herself five months, saying,

Thus hath the Lord dealt with me in the days wherein he looked on me, to take away my reproach among men.

And in the sixth month the angel Gabriel was sent from God unto a city of Galilee, named Nazareth,

To a virgin espoused to a man whose name was Joseph, of the house of David; and the virgin's name was Mary. . . .

And it came to pass, that, when Elisabeth heard the salutation of Mary, the babe leaped in her womb; and Elisabeth was filled with the Holy Ghost:

And she spake out with a loud voice, and said, Blessed art thou among women, and blessed is the fruit of thy womb.

And whence is this to me, that the mother of my Lord should come to me?

For, lo, as soon as the voice of thy salutation sounded in mine ears, the babe leaped in my womb for joy.

And blessed is she that believed: for there shall be a performance of those things which were told her from the Lord. . . .

Now Elisabeth's full time came that she should be delivered; and she brought forth a son.

And her neighbours and her cousins heard how the Lord had shewed great mercy upon her; and they rejoiced with her. . . .

And thou, child, shalt be called the prophet of the Highest: for thou shalt go before the face of the Lord to prepare his ways;

To give knowledge of salvation unto his people by the remission of their sins,

—*Luke 1:24–37, 41–45, 57–58, 76–77*

⋘ *Hannah: Samuel's Mother*

She was in bitterness of soul, and prayed unto the LORD, and wept sore.

And she vowed a vow, and said, O LORD of hosts, if thou wilt indeed look on the affliction of thine handmaid, and remember me, and not forget thine handmaid, but wilt give unto thine handmaid a man child, then I will give him unto the LORD all the days of his life, and there shall no razor come upon his head.

And it came to pass, as she continued praying before the LORD, that Eli marked her mouth.

Now Hannah, she spake in her heart; only her lips moved, but her voice was not heard: therefore Eli thought she had been drunken.

And Eli said unto her, How long wilt thou be drunken? put away thy wine from thee.

And Hannah answered and said, No, my lord, I am a woman of a sorrowful spirit: I have drunken neither wine nor strong drink, but have poured out my soul before the LORD.

Count not thine handmaid for a daughter of Belial: for out of the abundance of my complaint and grief have I spoken hitherto.

Then Eli answered and said, Go in peace: and the God of Israel grant thee thy petition that thou hast asked of him.

And she said, Let thine handmaid find grace in thy sight. So the woman went her way, and did eat, and her countenance was no more sad.

And they rose up in the morning early, and worshipped before the LORD, and returned, and came to their house to Ramah: and Elkanah knew Hannah his wife; and the LORD remembered her.

Wherefore it came to pass, when the time was come about after Hannah had conceived, that she bare a son, and called his name Samuel, saying, Because I have asked him of the LORD.

And the man Elkanah, and all his house, went up to offer unto the LORD the yearly sacrifice, and his vow.

But Hannah went not up; for she said unto her husband, I will not go up until the child be weaned, and then I will bring him, that he may appear before the LORD, and there abide for ever.

And Elkanah her husband said unto her, Do what seemeth thee good; tarry until thou have weaned him; only the LORD establish his word. So the woman abode, and gave her son suck until she weaned him.

And when she had weaned him, she took him up with her, with three bullocks, and one ephah of flour, and a bottle of wine, and brought him unto the house of the LORD in Shiloh: and the child was young.

And they slew a bullock, and brought the child to Eli.

And she said, Oh my lord, as thy soul liveth, my lord, I am the woman that stood by thee here, praying unto the LORD.

For this child I prayed; and the LORD hath given me my petition which I asked of him:

Therefore also I have lent him to the LORD; as long as he liveth he shall be lent to the LORD. And he worshipped the LORD there.

—*1 Samuel 1:10–28*

Hannah prayed, and said, My heart rejoiceth in the LORD, mine horn is exalted in the LORD: my mouth is enlarged over mine enemies; because I rejoice in thy salvation.

There is none holy as the LORD: for there is none beside thee: neither is there any rock like our God.

Talk no more so exceeding proudly; let not arrogancy come out of your mouth: for the LORD is a God of knowledge, and by him actions are weighed.

The bows of the mighty men are broken, and they that stumbled are girded with strength.

They that were full have hired out themselves for bread; and they that were hungry ceased: so that the barren hath born seven; and she that hath many children is waxed feeble.

The LORD killeth, and maketh alive: he bringeth down to the grave, and bringeth up.

The LORD maketh poor, and maketh rich: he bringeth low, and lifteth up.

He raiseth up the poor out of the dust, and lifteth up the beggar from the dunghill, to set them among princes, and to make them inherit the throne of glory: for the pillars of the earth are the LORD's, and he hath set the world upon them.

He will keep the feet of his saints, and the wicked shall be silent in darkness; for by strength shall no man prevail.

The adversaries of the LORD shall be broken to pieces; out of heaven shall he thunder upon them: the LORD shall judge the ends of the earth; and he shall give strength unto his king, and exalt the horn of his anointed. . . .

And the LORD visited Hannah, so that she conceived, and bare three sons and two daughters. And the child Samuel grew before the LORD.

—*1 Samuel 2:1–10, 21*

⋘ *Mary: Jesus' Mother*

In the sixth month the angel Gabriel was sent from God unto a city of Galilee, named Nazareth,

To a virgin espoused to a man whose name was Joseph, of the house of David; and the virgin's name was Mary.

And the angel came in unto her, and said, Hail, thou that art highly favoured, the Lord is with thee: blessed art thou among women.

And when she saw him, she was troubled at his saying, and cast in her mind what manner of salutation this should be.

And the angel said unto her, Fear not, Mary: for thou hast found favour with God.

And, behold, thou shalt conceive in thy womb, and bring forth a son, and shalt call his name JESUS. . . .

And Mary said, My soul doth magnify the Lord,

And my spirit hath rejoiced in God
my Saviour.

For he hath regarded the low estate of his
handmaiden: for, behold, from henceforth all
generations shall call me blessed.

For he that is mighty hath done to me great
things; and holy is his name.

And his mercy is on them that fear him
from generation to generation.

He hath shewed strength with his arm; he
hath scattered the proud in the imagination
of their hearts.

He hath put down the mighty from their
seats, and exalted them of low degree.

He hath filled the hungry with good things;
and the rich he hath sent empty away.

—*Luke 1:26–31, 46–53*

⋘ *Sarah: Mother of Isaac*

God said unto Abraham, As for Sarai thy
wife, thou shalt not call her name Sarai, but
Sarah shall her name be.

And I will bless her, and give thee a son also
of her: yea, I will bless her, and she shall be a
mother of nations; kings of people shall be
of her.

Then Abraham fell upon his face, and laughed, and said in his heart, Shall a child be born unto him that is an hundred years old? and shall Sarah, that is ninety years old, bear?

And Abraham said unto God, O that Ishmael might live before thee!

And God said, Sarah thy wife shall bear thee a son indeed; and thou shalt call his name Isaac: and I will establish my covenant with him for an everlasting covenant, and with his seed after him. . . .

And they said unto him, Where is Sarah thy wife? And he said, Behold, in the tent.

And he said, I will certainly return unto thee according to the time of life; and, lo, Sarah thy wife shall have a son. And Sarah heard it in the tent door, which was behind him.

Now Abraham and Sarah were old and well stricken in age; and it ceased to be with Sarah after the manner of women.

Therefore Sarah laughed within herself, saying, After I am waxed old shall I have pleasure, my lord being old also?

And the LORD said unto Abraham, Wherefore did Sarah laugh, saying, Shall I of a surety bear a child, which am old?

Is any thing too hard for the LORD? At the time appointed I will return unto thee, according to the time of life, and Sarah shall have a son. . . .

And the LORD visited Sarah as he had said, and the LORD did unto Sarah as he had spoken.

For Sarah conceived, and bare Abraham a son in his old age, at the set time of which God had spoken to him.

And Abraham called the name of his son that was born unto him, whom Sarah bare to him, Isaac.

—Genesis 17:15–19; 18:9–14; 21:1–3

⋘ *The Widow with Two Sons*

Now there cried a certain woman of the wives of the sons of the prophets unto Elisha, saying, Thy servant my husband is dead; and thou knowest that thy servant did fear the LORD: and the creditor is come to take unto him my two sons to be bondmen.

And Elisha said unto her, What shall I do for thee? tell me, what hast thou in the house? And she said, Thine handmaid hath not any thing in the house, save a pot of oil.

Then he said, Go, borrow thee vessels abroad of all thy neighbours, even empty vessels; borrow not a few.

And when thou art come in, thou shalt shut the door upon thee and upon thy sons, and shalt pour out into all those vessels, and thou shalt set aside that which is full.

So she went from him, and shut the door upon her and upon her sons, who brought the vessels to her; and she poured out.

And it came to pass, when the vessels were full, that she said unto her son, Bring me yet a vessel. And he said unto her, There is not a vessel more. And the oil stayed.

Then she came and told the man of God. And he said, Go, sell the oil, and pay thy debt, and live thou and thy children of the rest.

—2 Kings 4:1–7

So . . . Obey God, and Do Good!

Our families can survive with less of what we do. They just can't get by with less of what we give them out of who we are. Maybe we can't "do it all." But we can still give our families our hearts. We can turn our houses into homes, our families into, well, families. And one of the ways we can do it is by cherishing, not relegating, our special place as women, wives, and mothers in our homes.

—*Karen Scalf Linamen*[2]

And a certain woman named Lydia, a seller of purple, of the city of Thyatira, which worshipped God, heard us: whose heart the Lord opened, that she attended unto the things which were spoken of Paul.

And when she was baptized, and her household, she besought us, saying, If ye have judged me to be faithful to the Lord, come into my house, and abide there. And she constrained us.

—*Acts 16:14–15*

For to me to live is Christ, and to die is gain.

—*Philippians 1:21*

Now there was at Joppa a certain disciple named Tabitha, which by interpretation is called Dorcas: this woman was full of good works and almsdeeds which she did.

And it came to pass in those days, that she was sick, and died: whom when they had washed, they laid her in an upper chamber.

And forasmuch as Lydda was nigh to Joppa, and the disciples had heard that Peter was there, they sent unto him two men, desiring him that he would not delay to come to them.

Then Peter arose and went with them. When he was come, they brought him into the upper chamber: and all the widows stood by him weeping, and shewing the coats and garments which Dorcas made, while she was with them.

But Peter put them all forth, and kneeled down, and prayed; and turning him to the body said, Tabitha, arise. And she opened her eyes: and when she saw Peter, she sat up.

And he gave her his hand, and lifted her up, and when he had called the saints and widows, presented her alive.

And it was known throughout all Joppa; and many believed in the Lord.

—Acts 9:36–42

Nine

Praying Always

Why is it always easier to do everything else but pray? Learning to carve out space for talking to the Lord—and listening for Him—is the challenge of a lifetime. But we do need prayer. Without an intimate connection with God, we can hardly hope to survive our daily battles. Our prayerfulness expresses a moment-by-moment attitude of dependence upon Him, in all circumstances.

Learning to Pray . . .

We all come to prayer with a tangled mass of motives—altruistic and selfish, merciful and hateful, loving and bitter. Frankly, this side of eternity we will never unravel the good from the bad, the loving and bitter. But what I have come to see is that God is big enough to receive us with all our mixture. We do not have to be bright, or pure, or filled with faith, or anything. That is what grace means, and not only are we saved by grace, we live by it as well. And we pray by it.

—Richard Foster [1]

Pray without ceasing.

—1 Thessalonians 5:17

Yet have thou respect unto the prayer of thy servant, and to his supplication, O LORD my God, to hearken unto the cry and to the prayer, which thy servant prayeth before thee to day:

That thine eyes may be open toward this house night and day, even toward the place of which thou hast said, My name shall be there: that thou mayest hearken unto the prayer which thy servant shall make toward this place.

And hearken thou to the supplication of thy servant, and of thy people Israel, when they shall pray toward this place: and hear thou in heaven thy dwelling place: and when thou hearest, forgive.

—1 Kings 8:28–30

Thou shalt make thy prayer unto him, and he shall hear thee, and thou shalt pay thy vows.

Thou shalt also decree a thing, and it shall be established unto thee: and the light shall shine upon thy ways.

—Job 22:27–28

And when thou prayest, thou shalt not be as the hypocrites are: for they love to pray standing in the synagogues and in the corners of the streets, that they may be seen of men. Verily I say unto you, They have their reward.

But thou, when thou prayest, enter into thy closet, and when thou hast shut thy door, pray to thy Father which is in secret; and thy Father which seeth in secret shall reward thee openly.

But when ye pray, use not vain repetitions, as the heathen do: for they think that they shall be heard for their much speaking.

Be not ye therefore like unto them: for your Father knoweth what things ye have need of, before ye ask him.

After this manner therefore pray ye: Our Father which art in heaven, Hallowed be thy name.

Thy kingdom come. Thy will be done in earth, as it is in heaven.

Give us this day our daily bread.

And forgive us our debts, as we forgive our debtors.

And lead us not into temptation, but deliver us from evil: For thine is the kingdom, and the power, and the glory, for ever. Amen.

—*Matthew 6:5–13*

Verily I say unto you, Whatsoever ye shall bind on earth shall be bound in heaven: and whatsoever ye shall loose on earth shall be loosed in heaven.

—*Matthew 18:18*

Be careful for nothing; but in every thing by prayer and supplication with thanksgiving let your requests be made known unto God.

—*Philippians 4:6*

Let us therefore come boldly unto the throne of grace, that we may obtain mercy, and find grace to help in time of need.

—*Hebrews 4:16*

Let us draw near with a true heart in full assurance of faith, having our hearts sprinkled from an evil conscience, and our bodies washed with pure water.

—*Hebrews 10:22*

But without faith it is impossible to please him: for he that cometh to God must believe that he is, and that he is a rewarder of them that diligently seek him.

—*Hebrews 11:6*

And whatsoever we ask, we receive of him, because we keep his commandments, and do those things that are pleasing in his sight.

—*1 John 3:22*

These things have I written unto you that believe on the name of the Son of God; that ye may know that ye have eternal life, and that ye may believe on the name of the Son of God.

And this is the confidence that we have in him, that, if we ask any thing according to his will, he heareth us:

And if we know that he hear us, whatsoever we ask, we know that we have the petitions that we desired of him.

—1 John 5:13–15

Praying for Deliverance

O Lord, sea of love and goodness,
let me not fear too much the storms and winds
of my daily life,
and let me know that there is
ebb and flow
but that the sea remains the sea.

—*Henri Nouwen* [2]

There arose a great storm of wind, and the waves beat into the ship, so that it was now full.

And he was in the hinder part of the ship, asleep on a pillow: and they awake him, and say unto him, Master, carest thou not that we perish?

And he arose, and rebuked the wind, and said unto the sea, Peace, be still. And the wind ceased, and there was a great calm.

And he said unto them, Why are ye so fearful? how is it that ye have no faith?

—*Mark 4:37–39*

Therefore thus saith the LORD concerning the king of Assyria, He shall not come into this city, nor shoot an arrow there, nor come before it with shields, nor cast a bank against it.

By the way that he came, by the same shall he return, and shall not come into this city, saith the LORD.

—*Isaiah 37:33–34*

O wretched man that I am! who shall deliver me from the body of this death?

I thank God through Jesus Christ our Lord. So then with the mind I myself serve the law of God; but with the flesh the law of sin.

—*Romans 7:24–25*

Praying for Guidance

Part of the Spirit's gift is discernment. If we are to pray for ourselves and others according to the mind of Christ, we need to be led by the Spirit to know what to pray for and how and when. Jesus, too, had to pray for discernment; His mind was subjected to the Spirit, not automatically, but through prayer. He needed to soak Himself in the Father's presence and sensitize Himself to the Father's will.

—*Maria Boulding*[3]

Man's goings are of the LORD; how can a man then understand his own way?

—*Proverbs 20:24*

Thus saith the LORD, thy Redeemer, the Holy One of Israel; I am the LORD thy God which teacheth thee to profit, which leadeth thee by the way that thou shouldest go.

O that thou hadst hearkened to my commandments! then had thy peace been as a river, and thy righteousness as the waves of the sea.

—*Isaiah 48:17–18*

Behold, the days come, saith the Lord GOD, that I will send a famine in the land, not a famine of bread, nor a thirst for water, but of hearing the words of the LORD:

And they shall wander from sea to sea, and from the north even to the east, they shall run to and fro to seek the word of the LORD, and shall not find it.

—Amos 8:11–12

Thy word is a lamp unto my feet, and a light unto my path. . . .

I am thy servant; give me understanding, that I may know thy testimonies.

—Psalm 119:105, 125

Now there were in the church that was at Antioch certain prophets and teachers; as Barnabas, and Simeon that was called Niger, and Lucius of Cyrene, and Manaen, which had been brought up with Herod the tetrarch, and Saul.

As they ministered to the Lord, and fasted, the Holy Ghost said, Separate me Barnabas and Saul for the work whereunto I have called them.

And when they had fasted and prayed, and laid their hands on them, they sent them away.

—*Acts 13:1–3*

Then spake the Lord to Paul in the night by a vision, Be not afraid, but speak, and hold not thy peace:

For I am with thee, and no man shall set on thee to hurt thee: for I have much people in this city.

And he continued there a year and six months, teaching the word of God among them.

—*Acts 18:9–11*

Praying for Wisdom

Everyone is naturally contemplative. The people we call contemplatives are not unique in their nature; they just have a little extra longing to recover the nature that is common to us all. Scripture tells us that we must become like little children, and that the teaching we need is right here if we have eyes to see and ears to hear. It tells us that we live and move and have our being in a divine One who is already at home is us, ready to guide us where we need to go. It tells us that Holy Wisdom cries in the streets for us, promising that in self-abandonment we will never be abandoned. It assures us that we will find what we seek, that we shall know the truth, and that it will make us free.

—*Gerald May* [4]

If any of you lack wisdom, let him ask of God, that giveth to all men liberally, and upbraideth not; and it shall be given him.

But let him ask in faith, nothing wavering. For he that wavereth is like a wave of the sea driven with the wind and tossed.

For let not that man think that he shall
receive any thing of the Lord.

A double minded man is unstable in all
his ways.

—James 1:5–8

The fear of the LORD is the beginning of
wisdom: a good understanding have all they
that do his commandments: his praise
endureth for ever.

—Psalm 111:10

I am thy servant; give me understanding,
that I may know thy testimonies.

—Psalm 119:125

And when they bring you unto the synagogues, and unto magistrates, and powers,
take ye no thought how or what thing ye shall
answer, or what ye shall say:

For the Holy Ghost shall teach you in the
same hour what ye ought to say.

—Luke 12:11–12

For I will give you a mouth and wisdom,
which all your adversaries shall not be able to
gainsay nor resist.

—Luke 21:15

Consider what I say; and the Lord give thee understanding in all things.

—*2 Timothy 2:7*

And we know that the Son of God is come, and hath given us an understanding, that we may know him that is true, and we are in him that is true, even in his Son Jesus Christ. This is the true God, and eternal life.

—*1 John 5:20*

Praying for Others

He prayeth best who loveth best
All things both great and small;
For the dear God who loveth us,
He made and loveth all.

—*Samuel Taylor Coleridge*

And this I pray, that your love may abound yet more and more in knowledge and in all judgment.

—*Philippians 1:9*

For this cause we also, since the day we heard it, do not cease to pray for you, and to desire that ye might be filled with the knowledge of his will in all wisdom and spiritual understanding;

That ye might walk worthy of the Lord unto all pleasing, being fruitful in every good work, and increasing in the knowledge of God;

Strengthened with all might, according to his glorious power, unto all patience and longsuffering with joyfulness.

—*Colossians 1:9–11*

And Reuben heard it, and he delivered him out of their hands; and said, Let us not kill him.

And Reuben said unto them, Shed no blood, but cast him into this pit that is in the wilderness, and lay no hand upon him; that he might rid him out of their hands, to deliver him to his father again.

—*Genesis 37:21–22*

I beseech thee for my son Onesimus, whom I have begotten in my bonds:

Which in time past was to thee unprofitable, but now profitable to thee and to me.

—*Philemon 10–11*

Offering Praise and Thanks

God, I give You the praise for days well spent. But I am yet unsatisfied, because I do not enjoy enough of You. I apprehend myself at too great a distance from You.
I would have my soul more closely united to You by faith and love.

You know, Lord, that I would love You above all things. You made me, You know my desires, my expectations. My joys all center in You and it is You that I desire. It is Your favour, Your acceptance, the communication of Your grace that I earnestly wish for more than anything in the world.

I rejoice in Your essential glory and blessedness. I rejoice in my relation to You, that You are my Father, my Lord and my God. I thank You that You have brought me so far. I will beware of despairing of Your mercy for the time which is yet to come, and will give You the glory for Your free grace.

—*Susanna Wesley*

O come, let us worship and bow down: let us kneel before the LORD our maker.

—*Psalm 95:6*

I will sing of the mercies of the LORD for ever: with my mouth will I make known thy faithfulness to all generations.

For I have said, Mercy shall be built up for ever: thy faithfulness shalt thou establish in the very heavens.

I have made a covenant with my chosen, I have sworn unto David my servant,

Thy seed will I establish for ever, and build up thy throne to all generations. Selah.

—*Psalm 89:1–4*

The LORD shall increase you more and more, you and your children.

Ye are blessed of the LORD which made heaven and earth.

The heaven, even the heavens, are the LORD's: but the earth hath he given to the children of men.

The dead praise not the LORD, neither any that go down into silence.

But we will bless the LORD from this time forth and for evermore. Praise the LORD.

—*Psalm 115:14–18*

This is the day which the LORD hath made; we will rejoice and be glad in it.

—*Psalm 118:24*

I will extol thee, my God, O king; and I will bless thy name for ever and ever.

Every day will I bless thee; and I will praise thy name for ever and ever.

Great is the LORD, and greatly to be praised; and his greatness is unsearchable.

One generation shall praise thy works to another, and shall declare thy mighty acts.

—*Psalm 145:1–4*

Then saith Jesus unto him, Get thee hence, Satan: for it is written, Thou shalt worship the Lord thy God, and him only shalt thou serve.

—*Matthew 4:10*

Jesus saith unto her, Woman, believe me, the hour cometh, when ye shall neither in this mountain, nor yet at Jerusalem, worship the Father.

Ye worship ye know not what: we know what we worship: for salvation is of the Jews.

But the hour cometh, and now is, when the true worshippers shall worship the Father in spirit and in truth: for the Father seeketh such to worship him.

God is a Spirit: and they that worship him must worship him in spirit and in truth.

—John 4:21–24

Let the word of Christ dwell in you richly in all wisdom; teaching and admonishing one another in psalms and hymns and spiritual songs, singing with grace in your hearts to the Lord.

—Colossians 3:16

Learning from Your Master-Teacher

Where do you go for the best advice? When Jesus walked the earth, He not only provided the ultimate heavenly wisdom, He taught in the most interesting ways—so that His message would make the greatest impact for change. Learn from Him today, for, just as He did centuries ago, He still speaks directly to the heart.

He Taught in Parables

If you seek the kernel, then you must break the shell. And likewise, if you would know the reality of Nature, you must destroy the appearance, and the farther you go beyond the appearance, the nearer you will be to the essence.

—Meister Eckhart

Son of man, put forth a riddle, and speak a parable unto the house of Israel.

—Ezekiel 17:2

I will open my mouth in a parable: I will utter dark sayings of old.

—Psalm 78:2

And the disciples came, and said unto him, Why speakest thou unto them in parables? . . .

Therefore speak I to them in parables: because they seeing see not; and hearing they hear not, neither do they understand. . . .

All these things spake Jesus unto the multitude in parables; and without a parable spake he not unto them.

That it might be fulfilled which was spoken by the prophet, saying, I will open my mouth in parables; I will utter things which have been kept secret from the foundation of the world.

—*Matthew 13:10, 13, 34–35*

So Learn from Him . . .

Learn of the skillful; he that teaches himself,
hath a fool for his master.

—*Benjamin Franklin*

⋘ *About Forgiveness*

There was a certain creditor which had two debtors: the one owed five hundred pence, and the other fifty.

And when they had nothing to pay, he frankly forgave them both. Tell me therefore, which of them will love him most?

Simon answered and said, I suppose that he, to whom he forgave most. And he said unto him, Thou hast rightly judged.

And he turned to the woman, and said unto Simon, Seest thou this woman? I entered into thine house, thou gavest me no water for my feet: but she hath washed my feet with tears, and wiped them with the hairs of her head.

Thou gavest me no kiss: but this woman since the time I came in hath not ceased to kiss my feet.

My head with oil thou didst not anoint: but this woman hath anointed my feet with ointment.

Wherefore I say unto thee, Her sins, which are many, are forgiven; for she loved much: but to whom little is forgiven, the same loveth little.

—*Luke 7:41–47*

⋘ *About the Right Priorities*

And he spake a parable unto them, saying, The ground of a certain rich man brought forth plentifully:

And he thought within himself, saying, What shall I do, because I have no room where to bestow my fruits?

And he said, This will I do: I will pull down my barns, and build greater; and there will I bestow all my fruits and my goods.

And I will say to my soul, Soul, thou hast much goods laid up for many years; take thine ease, eat, drink, and be merry.

But God said unto him, Thou fool, this night thy soul shall be required of thee: then whose shall those things be, which thou hast provided?

So is he that layeth up treasure for himself, and is not rich toward God.

—Luke 12:16–21

⋘ *About Persistence*

He said unto them, Which of you shall have a friend, and shall go unto him at midnight, and say unto him, Friend, lend me three loaves;

For a friend of mine in his journey is come to me, and I have nothing to set before him?

And he from within shall answer and say, Trouble me not: the door is now shut, and my children are with me in bed; I cannot rise and give thee.

I say unto you, Though he will not rise and give him, because he is his friend, yet because of his importunity he will rise and give him as many as he needeth.

—Luke 11:5–8

About Responding to God's Grace

And when one of them that sat at meat with him heard these things, he said unto him, Blessed is he that shall eat bread in the kingdom of God.

Then said he unto him, A certain man made a great supper, and bade many:

And sent his servant at supper time to say to them that were bidden, Come; for all things are now ready.

And they all with one consent began to make excuse. The first said unto him, I have bought a piece of ground, and I must needs go and see it: I pray thee have me excused.

And another said, I have bought five yoke of oxen, and I go to prove them: I pray thee have me excused.

And another said, I have married a wife, and therefore I cannot come.

So that servant came, and shewed his lord these things. Then the master of the house being angry said to his servant, Go out quickly into the streets and lanes of the city, and bring in hither the poor, and the maimed, and the halt, and the blind.

And the servant said, Lord, it is done as thou hast commanded, and yet there is room.

And the lord said unto the servant, Go out into the highways and hedges, and compel them to come in, that my house may be filled.

For I say unto you, That none of those men which were bidden shall taste of my supper.

—*Luke 14:15–24*

≪ *About Interpersonal Justice*

He said also unto his disciples, There was a certain rich man, which had a steward; and the same was accused unto him that he had wasted his goods.

And he called him, and said unto him, How is it that I hear this of thee? give an account of thy stewardship; for thou mayest be no longer steward.

Then the steward said within himself, What shall I do? for my lord taketh away from me the stewardship: I cannot dig; to beg I am ashamed.

I am resolved what to do, that, when I am put out of the stewardship, they may receive me into their houses.

So he called every one of his lord's debtors unto him, and said unto the first, How much owest thou unto my lord?

And he said, An hundred measures of oil. And he said unto him, Take thy bill, and sit down quickly, and write fifty.

Then said he to another, And how much owest thou? And he said, An hundred measures of wheat. And he said unto him, Take thy bill, and write fourscore.

And the lord commended the unjust steward, because he had done wisely: for the children of this world are in their generation wiser than the children of light.

And I say unto you, Make to yourselves friends of the mammon of unrighteousness; that, when ye fail, they may receive you into everlasting habitations.

—Luke 16:1–9

⋘ *About Pride and Humility*

And he spake this parable unto certain which trusted in themselves that they were righteous, and despised others:

Two men went up into the temple to pray; the one a Pharisee, and the other a publican.

The Pharisee stood and prayed thus with himself, God, I thank thee, that I am not as other men are, extortioners, unjust, adulterers, or even as this publican.

I fast twice in the week, I give tithes of all that I possess.

And the publican, standing afar off, would not lift up so much as his eyes unto heaven, but smote upon his breast, saying, God be merciful to me a sinner.

I tell you, this man went down to his house justified rather than the other: for every one that exalteth himself shall be abased; and he that humbleth himself shall be exalted.

—Luke 18:9–14

⋘ *About Working in the Kingdom*

For the kingdom of heaven is like unto a man that is an householder, which went out early in the morning to hire labourers into his vineyard.

And when he had agreed with the labourers for a penny a day, he sent them into his vineyard.

And he went out about the third hour, and saw others standing idle in the marketplace,

And said unto them; Go ye also into the vineyard, and whatsoever is right I will give you. And they went their way.

Again he went out about the sixth and ninth hour, and did likewise.

And about the eleventh hour he went out, and found others standing idle, and saith unto them, Why stand ye here all the day idle?

They say unto him, Because no man hath hired us. He saith unto them, Go ye also into the vineyard; and whatsoever is right, that shall ye receive.

So when even was come, the lord of the vineyard saith unto his steward, Call the labourers, and give them their hire, beginning from the last unto the first.

And when they came that were hired about the eleventh hour, they received every man a penny.

But when the first came, they supposed that they should have received more; and they likewise received every man a penny.

And when they had received it, they murmured against the goodman of the house,

Saying, These last have wrought but one hour, and thou hast made them equal unto us, which have borne the burden and heat of the day.

But he answered one of them, and said, Friend, I do thee no wrong: didst not thou agree with me for a penny?

Take that thine is, and go thy way: I will give unto this last, even as unto thee.

Is it not lawful for me to do what I will with mine own? Is thine eye evil, because I am good?

So the last shall be first, and the first last: for many be called, but few chosen.

—*Matthew 20:1–16*

About Being Ready for Jesus

For the kingdom of heaven is as a man travelling into a far country, who called his own servants, and delivered unto them his goods.

And unto one he gave five talents, to another two, and to another one; to every man according to his several ability; and straightway took his journey.

Then he that had received the five talents went and traded with the same, and made them other five talents.

And likewise he that had received two, he also gained other two.

But he that had received one went and digged in the earth, and hid his lord's money.

After a long time the lord of those servants cometh, and reckoneth with them.

And so he that had received five talents came and brought other five talents, saying, Lord, thou deliveredst unto me five talents: behold, I have gained beside them five talents more.

His lord said unto him, Well done, thou good and faithful servant: thou hast been faithful over a few things, I will make thee ruler over many things: enter thou into the joy of thy lord.

He also that had received two talents came and said, Lord, thou deliveredst unto me two talents: behold, I have gained two other talents beside them.

His lord said unto him, Well done, good and faithful servant; thou hast been faithful over a few things, I will make thee ruler over many things: enter thou into the joy of thy lord.

Then he which had received the one talent came and said, Lord, I knew thee that thou art an hard man, reaping where thou hast not sown, and gathering where thou hast not strawed:

And I was afraid, and went and hid thy talent in the earth: lo, there thou hast that is thine.

His lord answered and said unto him, Thou wicked and slothful servant, thou knewest that I reap where I sowed not, and gather where I have not strawed:

Thou oughtest therefore to have put my money to the exchangers, and then at my coming I should have received mine own with usury.

Take therefore the talent from him, and give it unto him which hath ten talents.

For unto every one that hath shall be given, and he shall have abundance: but from him that hath not shall be taken away even that which he hath.

And cast ye the unprofitable servant into outer darkness: there shall be weeping and gnashing of teeth.

—Matthew 25:14–30

. . . And Follow Him Daily

To regard the career of Jesus as something far removed from the situation in which we live is to lose the encouragement that comes from viewing our fate in the light of His. If Jesus faced life as we have to face it, not walking through life "on spiritual stilts" but "in every respect . . . tempted as we are," then we can take heart both from His faithfulness and also from God's vindication of that faithfulness. . . .

If Jesus lived out His life amid the realities of the same world in which we live, then we too can face anything.

—*Eliot Porter*

Then he called his twelve disciples together, and gave them power and authority over all devils, and to cure diseases.

And he sent them to preach the kingdom of God, and to heal the sick.

And he said unto them, Take nothing for your journey, neither staves, nor scrip, neither bread, neither money; neither have two coats apiece.

And whatsoever house ye enter into, there abide, and thence depart.

And whosoever will not receive you, when ye go out of that city, shake off the very dust from your feet for a testimony against them.

—*Luke 9:1–5*

And he said to them all, If any man will come after me, let him deny himself, and take up his cross daily, and follow me.

For whosoever will save his life shall lose it: but whosoever will lose his life for my sake, the same shall save it.

For what is a man advantaged, if he gain the whole world, and lose himself, or be cast away?

—*Luke 9:23–25*

Jesus answered them, saying, The hour is come, that the Son of man should be glorified.

Verily, verily, I say unto you, Except a corn of wheat fall into the ground and die, it abideth alone: but if it die, it bringeth forth much fruit.

He that loveth his life shall lose it; and he that hateth his life in this world shall keep it unto life eternal.

If any man serve me, let him follow me; and where I am, there shall also my servant be: if any man serve me, him will my Father honour.

—*John 12:23–26*

So after he had washed their feet, and had taken his garments, and was set down again, he said unto them, Know ye what I have done to you?

Ye call me Master and Lord: and ye say well; for so I am.

If I then, your Lord and Master, have washed your feet; ye also ought to wash one another's feet.

For I have given you an example, that ye should do as I have done to you.

Verily, verily, I say unto you, The servant is not greater than his lord; neither he that is sent greater than he that sent him.

If ye know these things, happy are ye if ye do them.

—*John 13:12–17*

Little children, yet a little while I am with you. Ye shall seek me: and as I said unto the Jews, Whither I go, ye cannot come; so now I say to you.

A new commandment I give unto you, That ye love one another; as I have loved you, that ye also love one another.

By this shall all men know that ye are my disciples, if ye have love one to another.

Simon Peter said unto him, Lord, whither goest thou? Jesus answered him, Whither I go, thou canst not follow me now; but thou shalt follow me afterwards.

—*John 13:33–36*

Notes

—Chapter One—

1 Madeleine L'Engle, *Two-part Invention: The Story of a Marriage* (New York: Farrar, Straus and Giroux, 1988).

2 E. Paul Hovey, in *The Treasury of Inspirational Anecdotes, Quotations, and Illustrations* (Grand Rapids: Revell, 1987).

—Chapter Two—

1 Pearl S. Buck, quoted in William Safire and Leonard Safir, eds., *Words of Wisdom: More Good Advice* (New York, Simon and Schuster, 1990).

2 Burton Hillis, in *Better Homes & Gardens.*

3 William J. Bennett, in *The Book of Virtues* (New York: Simon and Schuster, 1993).

4 Dave Veerman, in *Parents and Children.*

—Chapter Three—

1 Jacob A. Riis, quoted in Hovey.

—Chapter Four—

1 Tim Hansel, in *What Kids Need Most in a Dad.*

—Chapter Five—

1 Erma Bombeck, *The Grass Is Always Greener over the Septic Tank,* as quoted in Annette LaPlaca, ed., *I Read It on the Refrigerator* (Wheaton, Ill: Harold Shaw, 1992).

2 James Dobson, in *Dare to Discipline.*

3 Edith Warton, in *A Backward Glance.*

4 C. S. Lewis, in *Mere Christianity* (New York: Macmillan, 1971).

—Chapter Six—

1 Michael Saward, in *The Complete Book of Christian Prayer* (New York: Continuum, 1995).

2 L'Engle, in *Two-Part Invention.*

3 Lewis, in *Mere Christianity.*

—Chapter Seven—

1 Christina Rossetti, in Robert Van deWeyer, ed., *The HarperCollins Book of Prayers* (San Francisco: HarperSanFrancisco, 1993).

2 Robert Murray M'Cheyne, in Stanley Barnes, comp., *God Makes a Path* (Belfast: Ambassador, 1995).

—Chapter Eight—

1 Peter Brown, in *Augustine of Hippo: A Biography* (Berkeley: University of California Press, 1967).

2 Karen Scalf Linamen, *Working Women, Workable Lives,* in *Women's Wisdom.*

—Chapter Nine—

1 Richard Foster, in *Prayer* (San Francisco: HarperCollins, 1992).

2 Henri Nouwen, in *the Harper Collins Book of Prayers* (San Francisco: HarperSanFrancisco, 1993).

3 Maria Boulding, *Marked for Life,* quoted in *The Complete Book of Christian Prayer* (New York: Continuum, 1995).

4 Gerald May in *The Shalem Newsletter,* vol. 18, no. 1.